June Callwood's
NATIONAL TREASURES

ALSO BY JUNE CALLWOOD

Love, Hate, Fear, and Anger   1964
Canadian Women and the Law, with Marvin Zuker   1973
The Law Is Not for Women, with Marvin Zuker   1975
Emma   1984
Portrait of Canada   1986
Twelve Weeks in Spring   1986
Emotions   1986
The Sleepwalker   1990

June Callwood's
NATIONAL
TREASURES

Stoddart

VISION/TV

Co-published in 1994 by
Stoddart Publishing Co. Limited
34 Lesmill Road
Toronto, Canada
M3B 2T6
(416) 445-3333

Vision TV
315 Queen Street East
Toronto, Canada
M5A 1S7

Canadian Cataloguing in Publication Data

Callwood, June
June Callwood's national treasures

Co-published by Vision TV.
ISBN 0-7737-5687-6

1. Canadians — Interviews. I. Vision TV. II. Title

FC601.A1C35 1994   971.064′092′2   C94-931835-3
F1034.3.A2C35 1994

Cover Design: Bill Douglas/The Bang
Printed in Canada

*Stoddart Publishing gratefully acknowledges the support of
the Canada Council, Ontario Ministry of Culture, Tourism,
and Recreation, Ontario Arts Council, and
Ontario Publishing Centre in the development of
writing and publishing in Canada.*

Contents

NATIONAL
TREASURES

Introduction

VISION TV, a channel renowned for its all-faiths and multiracial programming, is appropriately located in a shabby old Toronto church that sits among small, dejected shops and shelters for the homeless. With its exceedingly modest budget, Vision is obliged, like its neighbours, to be frugal. The interior of the sooty old church on Queen Street East has been partitioned into a maze of tiny offices furnished with mismatched castoffs where numerous cheerful people work industriously. I went there one bitterly cold March day in 1991 to talk about the possibility of being part of this crazy shoestring operation that was attracting a growing audience of Canadians, who are astonished by its freshness, idealism, and sincerity.

In a tacky room somewhere in the rear of the building, I met with Peter Flemington, an urbane and charming man who seems to decide programming at Vision; Jim Hanley, a big restless person with thinning grey hair tied back in a tight ponytail whom many believe to be a true genius of television; and Jacqueline Barley, a wry, attractive, self-effacing, immensely competent woman who works for Jim Hanley's Sleeping Giant Productions. They asked me if I had an idea for a television series I might do for Vision, and I told them about Eric Arthur.

Eric Arthur was in his late 70s when I met him at a lunch hosted by an old friend, Janet Tupper Underwood. She thought we would get along and indeed we did: the friendship lasted until his death 10 years later. Eric Arthur was a much-respected academic and architect, passionately concerned about conservancy, who contributed hugely to the look of Toronto. For instance, the restoration of St. Lawrence Hall is entirely his endeavour and he chaired the jury that chose the plans for the new City Hall. What I prized in him, besides his personal elegance and distinguished mind, was his prowess as a conversationalist. Over a decade of lunches, he regaled me with stories of famous people he knew and buildings he detested, providing me on the way with an education in cityscape appreciation. It was Eric Arthur who directed my attention to manhole covers which, he said, expressed the individuality and artistry of ironworkers.

I often wished that I had taken a tape recorder to our meetings or, better still, a camera crew. What he had to say was social history at its finest, and I regretted that Eric's stories of his involvement with momentous issues would be lost with his death. What I said that March day at Vision was that I wished to preserve on tape Canadian treasures like Eric Arthur whose notable contributions to the sanity and richness of this country should not be lost.

"Japan designates some of its citizens as 'national treasures' and they are accorded certain privileges," I explained. "Canada has the Order of Canada, which is something the same, but people don't really get to know much about the recipients. I'd like to be an archivist of sorts and show how these people put their lives together in ways that make the world a better place."

Who did I have in mind? Flemington asked. Well, I said, there was Senator David Croll, for one. After a long and distinguished career in politics, he had thrown himself into activities to relieve poverty despite his great age. I had some other names: Claire Culhane, a prison activist who lives in Vancouver; Pauline McGibbon, former lieutenant governor of Ontario; Art Solomon, a native elder; Peter Gzowski, whose CBC radio show *Morningside* stitches English Canada together; author Margaret Atwood; Sister Mary Jo Leddy, a nun caught up in the plight of refugees; and some more. What I would like to do, I explained, is explore how such people developed their ethic: why they made good choices about what to do with their lives.

Jim Hanley, who with Peter Flemington would be executive producers of the show for Vision, thought the idea had possibilities. Flemington agreed but wondered what my criteria would be for choosing a "Canadian treasure."

I went home and drew up the following: 1) The person is known nationally. 2) The person is respected. 3) There is something special about the way the person lives his or her life (not what the person does). 4) The person has a thought-out, as opposed to random and reactive, existence. 5) The person is able to define himself or herself.

Peter Flemington responded with some well-considered observations. He didn't think much of the requirement that subjects be known nationally. "We're trying to do a sort of *alternate* 'national treasures,'" he explained in a memo to Jim Hanley, which was passed on to me. "I think that these persons will not necessarily be known widely . . . they *will* become national treasures for reasons which, upon viewing, will become amply clear. We're talking about 'revelation' here."

He added: "Vision was required because television has progressively shied away from the depth dimension. As an industry, it's been embarrassed by words like faith, ethic, morality, and so on. Our weekly reach is by now well over the three-million mark because people are hungry for an affirmation that these things matter."

Peter reminded me that Vision concerns itself with spiritual matters. He hoped the people I interviewed would be able to discuss their relationship with God. That was fine with me: I'm still struggling to construct my own faith and I am curious about other people's progress on the same journey.

Jacqui Barley called a few weeks later. Since Vision had no studios, she had been scouting a location for the interviews. She found a charming Parkdale coach house in the rear of a heritage home. It was rented by Sonya Côté and Mark Gibson, friends of hers who were willing to allow their living room to be turned into a temporary television studio. Jacqui said the space was lovely, with a high ceiling, whitewashed walls, hanging plants, a wood-burning stove, and French doors that opened onto a garden. She planned to rent a grand piano for atmosphere, bring in fake flowers, and frame some posters for the walls. She was shopping for chairs for me and the guest. Did I like wicker? I love wicker, I assured her.

I was making lists of people I consider to be treasures. In consultation with Jim Hanley, Jacqui, and Peter Flemington, we made our choices from some 30 names I submitted. Liberated from the requirement that they be famous, I included friends who are little known outside their own circles but are putting their lives to good use. It was like assembling the best dinner party of your life. Peter Flemington approved them without a moment's hesitation.

Peter's willingness to take a chance no longer surprises me. When we met after the first season of *National Treasures* to discuss subjects for a second season, I told him I had just been to Kingston to visit some prisons, where I met a poet, John Rives, who was serving a life sentence for murder. I said, "I think John would make a good national treasure. To me he represents the beauty of redemption."

Peter didn't blink. "Good," he said. "Let's get him."

Here's a good place to thank Vision TV for its faith in me. I was in my late 60s when the series began, which I think made me one of the oldest female television hosts on the planet. Although Peter and Jim were far too tactful to ever discuss this factor, I rejoiced in the opportunity to show the wrinkled face of a truly old woman. An aged man who hosts a television show is considered distinguished, but an aged woman seems to invite derision. Old women appear on television mainly as props in commercials about tea or dentures. I hoped my weathered face and sagging jawline would make it easier for other old women to surmount the barriers.

In television terms a season is usually 13 shows or 26 shows. For reasons that were never clear to any of us, my first season on Vision consisted of something in between: 18 shows. We wanted a balance between men and women, so that factor influenced some of the decisions. Jacqui Barley did the tedious, frustrating chore of making the contacts and trying to adjust the schedules of very busy people to our shooting dates. Some people, like Rick Hansen, simply couldn't find the time; others, like Oscar Peterson, weren't available because of illness.

Eventually we were ready to start with a distinguished group: John Flannery, then director of nurses at Toronto's Casey House Hospice for people in the terminal stages of AIDS; Nancy White, the singer and songwriter, selected for her generous heart and commitment to good causes; Bob White, then head of Canadian Auto Workers, a principled and caring man; Pauline McGibbon, first woman lieutenant governor of a province and first woman chancellor of a university, greatly admired for her common sense and graciousness; Rosemary Brown, an outstanding feminist and crusader for human rights; Maureen Forrester, the glorious singer; Ovide Mercredi, newly elected chief of the Assembly of First Nations; Timothy Findley, novelist and one of the most charming people I know; Audrey King, a valiant and funny psychologist who has used a wheelchair most of her life; Peter Gzowski, who needs no introduction; Pat Capponi, who spent a great deal of time in psychiatric institutions and then became an author and an activist in the cause of housing the homeless; Pierre Berton, the most recognized person in the country, and deservedly so; Karen Kain, the elegant and exquisite dancer with an international reputation; Robert Munsch, who writes the world's most popular books for children; Clayton Ruby, brilliant criminal lawyer who throws himself headlong into freedom-of-speech issues; Claire Culhane, who corresponds with a thousand prisoners all over the country and tries to shield them from abuse; Lesley Parrott, who has been helping other bereaved parents since her 11-year-old daughter's brutal murder; and Gregory Baum, a former Augustinian priest and one of the architects of Vatican II.

The plan was to tape two interviews a day and, usually, leave the set in place in order to tape two more the next day. We began on August 6, 1991, with John Flannery of Casey House Hospice. The hospice opened in March 1988, and by the time of the interview had seen almost 300 deaths.

John's face shows the pain of so much loss but also the serenity and strength of a surpassingly good man. We were both nervous, but we have been friends a long time and eventually we relaxed. The second interview of the day was with Nancy White, the folk singer, songwriter, and generous person, who arrived after lunch and filled the room with her sparkle.

Jim Hanley squeezed himself behind a blanket hung in a corner where the production staff huddled. He watched the show on monitors, quietly approving the judgement and resourcefulness of Dan Robinson, the director.

Jim's signature on all his shows is the mood he establishes by the use of subtle lighting, tight close-ups, and interesting, homey backgrounds. He and Dan Robinson were delighted with the look of the show, which owed much to Jacqui Barley's good taste, but the old coach house presented a technical problem that alarmed everyone. Every time the cameras moved on the rubber-coated track, floorboards creaked. Dan's solution was to keep a roaring fire in the stove to make audiences think the noises were the crackle of burning wood. He was oblivious to my wail that we were taping these shows in the sweltering heat of August. Since our guests arrived in summer clothes and visibly sweated throughout the interview, the fire made no sense, I said. Yes, it did, he said pleasantly; he is a good-natured young man.

The compromise was that we kept the fire. Jacqui applied ice packs to the back of the neck of those guests who appeared ready to faint, assuring us all that this was the fastest way to cool the blood. On the blistering hot day when I interviewed

Pauline McGibbon, a woman of matchless dignity, Jacqui ran out of ice. She improvised by using a bag of frozen peas. Pauline, who is inflappable, only chuckled.

We had completed about six shows when I summoned the nerve to ask Jim Hanley what he thought of the interviews. He considered my question for a while, a toothpick in the corner of his mouth, then said, "Well, they aren't interviews."

"What are they?" I asked anxiously.

He gave this more thought. "I think what you are doing, June," he said gently, "is having a conversation. Don't panic. It'll work out."

It wasn't as though I hadn't prepared in the traditional way for the interview, studying the research and blocking out questions in some sort of order. My intention was to talk about the subject's career in the first segment of about 18 minutes, then use the next segment to trace the factors in early childhood that shaped the person's character and direction, and devote the final segment to an exploration of spiritual and ethical matters.

The problem with this sensible plan was that my guests could not be so neatly compartmentalized. Sometimes, checking my notes in the intervals when the cameramen changed tapes, I would find that almost none of my questions had been answered or, worse, that we had covered everything in my outline but 18 minutes still remained in the show.

Jim asked me to write an introduction that could run at the beginning of every show. I discovered when I sat down to do it that I had been asked to define what the series was all about. What emerged, after a great deal of staring out the window, is really very simple.

"Every Canadian can make a list of people we consider national treasures. What I think most lists have in common is that the people we admire are those whose lives reflect a sense of responsibility for others. The human race would not have survived if some people did not take up the struggle against what Gandhi described as 'untruth, injustice, and humbug.' In this series you'll meet some of the people I think exemplify a good life, a useful life. The givers. The treasures."

And here are some of them . . .

Margaret Atwood

$\mathcal{M}$argaret Atwood lives in a handsome big brick house in Toronto with Graeme Gibson, a novelist of military bearing and a lively social conscience, and their teenage daughter, Jess. Margaret is always writing: her output is prodigious, approximately a book a year for a total of more than 20 books. Some are poetry, some are essays, others collections of short stories; eight are novels. Translated into 20-some languages, she stuns the world with the sharpness of her observation and the lucidity of her language.

She is in huge demand to give readings, which she does in a flat, uninflected voice that astonishes audiences. Some years ago one young man in an auditorium at York University had the temerity to inquire why she reads that way. She replied evenly, "I am not an actress."

Because her face is composed and the gaze from her pale blue eyes can be piercing, many people find her intimidating. Often reporters begin their stories about Margaret Atwood by saying how frightened they were at the prospect of interviewing her, and how relieved they were to find her friendly and unassuming.

She's also funny. Her sense of the comic is acute and can be seen in the unexpected words she drops into her sparse, dry sentences. That gift of jolting people with an unanticipated response has served her in many circumstances. In a send-up of politically correct language, she avoided either *chairperson* or *chair* when she headed the Writers' Union of Canada, electing to call herself *chair-thing*. When she was president of the Canadian Centre of PEN International,

Margaret chaired an annual meeting that became disruptive. An indignant member complained about the failure of PEN to coordinate its annual general meeting with that of the Writers' Union of Canada so that out-of-town writers could attend both. It was a good point, and the two meetings have been in alignment ever since, but the person went on too long about it and expressed more outrage than the situation absolutely required. When the tirade ended, a silence fell. People waited for President Atwood to respond. President Atwood smiled serenely and said, "Fiddle-dee-dee."

Margaret Atwood won a Governor General's Award in 1966 for *The Circle Game*, a book of poetry, and has been winning awards ever since, including the prestigious Molson Award. *Survival*, an examination of the themes in Canadian literature, is a seminal piece of analysis, and it was followed with a cascade of children's books, novels, short stories, and literary criticism, all of them radiating from Atwood's fierce conscience.

Despite her prodigious output as a writer, she has been extraordinarily influential in the development of such organizations as House of Anansi Press, the Writers' Union of Canada, and the Canadian Centre of PEN International. She teems with fund-raising ideas, such as the *Eclectic Typewriter Review*, which raised money for the Writers' Union, and a cookbook she edited for PEN.

At the endless meetings that these activities entail, she's the cheerful, optimistic, inventive one. Like Judy Garland in the barn, it is Margaret Atwood who cries, "Hey gang, let's put on a show!" And put on a show she does, a world-class one.

CALLWOOD: I'd like to begin by talking about your involvement with various literary organizations. When you're weighing the cost of that, is the cost a book that you would have finished, if you hadn't been otherwise occupied?

ATWOOD: You never know what you would have done otherwise, but let us just say that because the Canadian writing community is small, everybody takes their turn sooner or later. So you say, I did it for a year, but that meant that somebody else did it for 19 other years with the Writers' Union, and other people have done it with PEN. It's like giving blood: you go down to the clinic, you roll up your sleeve, and give your blood. But you can't give all of your blood or else you would be dead. So you have to pick and choose what you will do, and you have to save some of your blood for yourself.

CALLWOOD: PEN was a bigger undertaking, though. When you came onto the scene, you found that it was going to pieces and knew it would take not just a few months but a couple of years out of your life.

ATWOOD: Did I know? Did I know that *(laughs)*?

CALLWOOD: Oh, you didn't know?

ATWOOD: Of course not. No, I was in England at the time and I got a letter from Constance Beresford-Howe, and what had happened was that PEN had been one organization, French and

English, in Montreal. Then it had divided into an English PEN and a French PEN — English-speaking and French-speaking. The English-speaking people in Montreal realized that if it remained there, it would die out, so they knew that they had to move it to Toronto. Constance Beresford-Howe took it on and found that they only had about seven active members. So she wrote to me in England and said, would I take it on? I said I would take it on if writers in prison was a priority, because I didn't see running a tea party organization. When I got back, I found that, in fact, there was no budget and that there were practically no members west of Toronto and practically none east of Montreal. So it wasn't really a national organization. Being a rather lazy person with very little energy, I phoned up the man that I knew could help me. His name is Eugene Benson. He is a whiz. He came in as co-chair and we increased the size and raised the money and —

CALLWOOD: Met in your living room for about two years.

ATWOOD: In the living room, in the dining room.

CALLWOOD: Standing up in the kitchen *(laughs)*.

ATWOOD: Those kinds of things. We had no staff or anybody, and finally under Timothy Findley, who was not interested in licking stamps, we acquired enough money and the inclination to get a very good executive director called Jan Bauer. But at this point, I was no longer the president. I was the early person when it was very small.

CALLWOOD: You were catalytic in that. You also came up with the fund-raising idea that started to turn PEN around, which was that cookbook.

ATWOOD: You know, if I ever knew how much work these things were going to be, I would never do them.

CALLWOOD: The cookbook was such a great idea.

ATWOOD: It was a great idea, but it took a lot of time. Here again you say, Oh, isn't she wonderful! But it's never just she, as you know perfectly well. You can't do these things without other people and the person who helped me a lot with that was the editor, Mary Adachi, and Nancy Colbert, who agented it. She was still an agent then. She agented it for nothing, and HarperCollins bought it. So you can't do it without lots of people.

CALLWOOD: Yes, but it's the initial impulse. It's like starting the universe. There has to be the first Big Bang.

ATWOOD: You have this stupid time-consuming idea, and then other people help you realize it.

CALLWOOD: When Marian Engel was chairing the Writers' Union, she insisted that she was a chairman. Do you remember that?

ATWOOD: Yeah.

CALLWOOD: Now, chairman is politically incorrect, but you also thought it was pretty ludicrous to be chairperson. So you were a —

ATWOOD: I was many things.

CALLWOOD: Yes.

ATWOOD: But now it's chair. I think we finally settled on chair.

CALLWOOD: That's all right for small people. For big people, it's sofa *(laughs)*. No, but you called yourself chair.

ATWOOD: Chairette was one. I tried out a number. I think the gist of it was that we needed something but that none of these things would do ultimately. I think it's settled down now and it's chair.

CALLWOOD: No one would guess, from all those accounts of the things you did for PEN that you also write a book a year, sometimes more.

ATWOOD: Well, not quite. It looks like a lot when you see them all under the heading "other books by." But you have to add in how old I am, and then divide the number of books into the age.

CALLWOOD: Yes, but you started with such a boom. You do a book of poetry and it wins the Governor General's Award. Then you do a novel and it also gets a Governor General's Award.

ATWOOD: Just go back in time a little before that. I did write a book a year and they all got routinely rejected before about 1965. So before what looked like a boom, there were many years of bust, as it were.

CALLWOOD: I didn't know that. That's not part of the Margaret Atwood mythology. You wrote —

ATWOOD: Well, let's add it in. I started writing when I was 16. I mean, who was going to publish a book by a 17-year-old? Did I know? No, I just kept sending them in.

CALLWOOD: What was wrong with them, if you look at them now?

ATWOOD: Oh, they were bad *(laughs)*. It cheers you up a lot to go back and read early Tennyson or early Blake. Everybody has what they call juvenilia, and this was juvenilia. It was juvenile. What can I tell you? I'm glad it wasn't published, but at the time, of course, I would be very dejected.

CALLWOOD: Were they introspective?

ATWOOD: I don't know. When you're young, of course, you go through about a style every six months. So I went through my T. S. Eliot period. I had a lot of coffee cups and garbage cans. When I went through a period where everything had a rhyme scheme, I wrote lots of sonnets. I shouldn't say they were bad. They were promising for the age that I was, but I was very young.

CALLWOOD: When Timothy Findley was giving advice to writers, as you're always asked to, he said that the only answer is, write, write, write. So there you sit, a living monument to that.

ATWOOD: Write, write, write and read, read, read. Yes. I think one of my lowest moments was when my book of poetry, which ultimately did get published and did win the Governor

General's, got accepted and then, several weeks later, got rejected because there was a three-man editorial board and the third man had turned it down. So there I was. It was sort of like having your wedding broken off. I'd told all my friends *(laughs)*.

CALLWOOD: So you changed publishers, I guess. That has to be the end of that story.

ATWOOD: Changed *(laughs)*! We're talking about a time when there weren't very many publishers.

CALLWOOD: And first books of poetry didn't have a chance.

ATWOOD: First books of poetry were usually published in people's basements by themselves. And, indeed, so was mine. It was about seven pages — seven poems long. I set the type myself. This was before desktop publishing or computers. We had a little flatbed press, and you had to put each letter in backward. Because there was a shortage of *A*'s I had to print one poem and then disassemble it and set the next one *(laughs)*. The book sold for 50 cents. It had a print run of 200. I wish I'd kept 150 of them.

CALLWOOD: Yes, when you think how valuable those things are now.

ATWOOD: I can tell you exactly how valuable. Last I heard, they were going for $1,000.

CALLWOOD: My word!

ATWOOD: Silly old me. I can tell the genuine article because I glued the covers on with rubber cement, which, after time, I can tell you, falls apart *(laughs)*.

CALLWOOD: Irving Layton printed his own first books, too, and has the same regrets because they're now also extremely valuable.

ATWOOD: Well, everybody printed their own books then. It was what you did. In fact, it was about the only thing to do because there was no other way in except through the five — count them — little magazines in Canada.

CALLWOOD: One time nearly 20 years ago, you came on the television show that I was doing then with a handbag like you did today and set it where you could see it. You said, "There's a poem in it." I thought, Does she only make one copy? Is that what you used to do?

ATWOOD: It was probably a poem that hadn't been typed out yet. No, of course, once I had typed them out, I made more than one copy with that archaic substance called carbon paper *(laughs)*.

CALLWOOD: Mmm, so that really would have been the only copy then. The producer wanted to put it behind the camera, but you said, "No, there's a poem in it." And everyone was so full of reverence.

ATWOOD: Were they? Thank goodness.

CALLWOOD: You often seem to seek out retreats. For example, you moved to Alliston, where you did real farming. You are back from France. It seems as though you're protecting yourself that way. Can you only do that by imposing a physical distance?

ATWOOD: Well, it's wonderful when it happens but, of course, it's not possible all the time. The only other way is to set a kind of filter system between you and the incoming requests, because, as you know yourself, there are endless requests.

CALLWOOD: And they're all things that you might want to do.

ATWOOD: They're all worthy things. When you only get 10 requests a year, you can do nine of them. But when you get 1,000 you can still only do nine. So you spend a lot of your time saying no.

CALLWOOD: Does the screening device not work well when you're in Toronto? Do more things get through? Is that why every now and then you seem almost driven to get out of the country?

ATWOOD: Yes. Well, the wonderful thing about not being in the country is that the phone doesn't ring. You know yourself how much time you take talking on the phone. I don't know, I think there's another reason, because I used to go away even before I had this and that kind of input. I think that when you're writing a novel you almost get a better view if you're not in your own country. It's like standing back to look at a picture. You can almost see the picture better from a certain distance.

CALLWOOD: You write when you're a writer-in-residence. You've been in Alabama, Texas, Alberta, and Australia. Were you a writer-in-residence in Scotland?

ATWOOD: No, that was Graeme [Gibson]. He was the writer-in-residence. I was the person with the two-and-a-half-year-old daycare kids and mums at the Scottish daycare centre, where we all got colds all the time *(laughs)*.

CALLWOOD: Do you write when you're a writer-in-residence?

ATWOOD: Yes. I write all the time. You condense the other things that you're doing in order to leave time for the writing.

CALLWOOD: Your sentences are such that you couldn't take one word away. Is it through the process of pruning that you get to them?

ATWOOD: It's because I've already taken a lot of words away. You're quite right.

CALLWOOD: Yeah. You've cut them down to their hardest bones.

ATWOOD: Well, I think when you're working with a style like that what you have to say is, Does this have a reason for being here? If it doesn't, it has to come out.

CALLWOOD: Is it in the morning that you have the greatest clarity?

ATWOOD: Now I write in the mornings. I used to be a night writer.

CALLWOOD: Did you? That's hard to change around.

ATWOOD: It was a gradual process, but here's something else you'll know: little babies wake up at about 6:30 in the morning, and that's when you get up. They're daytime people. So I had to change that around. Also, when you're living by yourself, you can really keep your own hours pretty much. When I was a night person, I had day jobs. So I was working a day job and then I was writing in the evenings and at night.

CALLWOOD: You became a full-time writer in the early '70s.

ATWOOD: Nineteen seventy-two. It's engraved in gold in my mind.

CALLWOOD: Before that you were teaching.

ATWOOD: I was doing many different kinds of things.

CALLWOOD: When you are a writer-in-residence and the people gather around, what can you communicate about creativity?

ATWOOD: When you're working with a group of people who want to be writers, I think you have to look at who you're talking to, and what stage they're at, and, of course, you address the stage that they are at. There is a book that I like to suggest that not just every young writer but every young artist of any kind read. It's called *The Gift*, and it's by a man called Lewis Hyde, as in Dr. Jekyll and Mr. Hyde. What it really is about is creativity and how it gets passed on. It's a very interesting book. It's also about gift exchanges, as opposed to money exchange, and how gift exchange works in a different way. For instance, if I sell you an automobile, I give you the car, you give me the money. That's the end of the transaction. If I give you one, it's a whole different proposition. You owe me something back. Now, you may not owe it to me, but you owe it to something or somebody. So you have to pass the gift along in some other form, and what Lewis Hyde argues is that creativity does not belong in the realm of money exchange. You cannot put a value on "Ode to a Nightingale." You cannot say, How much is this worth? It belongs in the area of gift exchange. So, if you have received that, then you have to give something yourself, because a gift that is not passed along dies.

CALLWOOD: You're paying your dues, are you?

ATWOOD: That's one way of putting it, but I like his way better.

CALLWOOD: Well, it's more poetic. I want to talk now about you as a young child because of my profound conviction that this has everything to do with the adult being. As a little kid you spent the summers in the woods with your father, who liked to look at bugs. Is that when you developed the habit of being an observer?

ATWOOD: Well, yes, my father was a professional entomologist, so it was his career.

CALLWOOD: We're not talking about bugs here. We're talking about serious study.

ATWOOD: We're talking about insects that eat trees. He was a forest entomologist, so that meant that it wasn't just summers — it was spring, summers, and falls. We were in the bush during any time of insect activity when I was little. That meant no radio, no movies, no cities, no plays — none of those things. The book was the medium of entertainment. Books and writing and drawing. So that was an early habit, but I had a dark period between the ages of eight and 16 during which I wasn't writing at all *(laughter)*. I thought first of all that I would be a painter, and then your reality principle crept in. Then I thought I would be a dress designer, and the reality principle crept in even further. Finally, I realized that I was going to have to be a home economist, because there were only five careers for women in the guidance book. They were . . . let's see how good you are. This is 1952.

CALLWOOD: Nurse.

ATWOOD: Yes.

CALLWOOD: Secretary.

ATWOOD: Yes.

CALLWOOD: Home economist.

ATWOOD: Yes.

CALLWOOD: Teacher.

ATWOOD: Yes.

CALLWOOD: What's the fifth?

ATWOOD: Airline stewardess *(laughter)*. That was it. So, I thought, well, I guess I'd better be a home economist. As a result I went into home economics, which meant that I didn't go into typing, which meant that I've never learned to type. The one time I tried to teach myself I went at it so furiously that I got blisters. But there were always things that I wanted to type, so I had to look. Consequently I've never learned to type properly.

CALLWOOD: You might have been a wonderful writer and been famous, if you'd only learned.

ATWOOD: I could have been, yeah. That and driving a car.

CALLWOOD: When you said home economist, I remembered that I read about you doing something really wingy in home economics, like an opera or something.

ATWOOD: I didn't think it was wingy. I thought it was a way out of having to make stuffed animals. You see, there's a very practical side to my nature. It was grade 12 and we were supposed to do a special project. The teacher made the mistake of saying we could vote on it. This is what is always wrong with democracy. People actually do choose, and they don't always choose what the person thinks they're going to. So I, in fact, subverted the class and said, "Instead of making these stuffed animals, which look quite hard, let's do a home economics opera." So we voted on it and the teacher — I'm afraid she was very good on hams, but she did not have a great sense of humour — had to go along with it. She said, "All right, as long as it's on the subject of home economics." So it was — it was about fabrics. It was about Orlon, Nylon,

Dacron, three princesses who lived with their father, Old King Coal — C-O-A-L — because these fabrics are all coal derivatives. And along came a wandering knight whose name was Sir William Wooly, played by my friend Joan, in a beard made out of paper bags. He had a terrible problem, which was that he shrank from washing. So many songs were sung on this theme. He ended up marrying Orlon, and they produced a blend that had all the virtues of both fabrics. Thunderous applause.

CALLWOOD: Oh, and it had a moral, too!

ATWOOD: People still turn up in my life who were in this opera.

CALLWOOD: Well, I was in a minor opera of yours one time — the Farley Mowat Dancers. That was very good.

ATWOOD: It was very good, except I almost killed us all. I didn't realize how hard it was going to be —

CALLWOOD: To dance on snowshoes.

ATWOOD: Dancing on snowshoes on a hardwood floor.

CALLWOOD: Who were the Farley Mowat Dancers? Marian Engel.

ATWOOD: Yes, and Alma Lee, Judith Merrill.

CALLWOOD: Sylvia Fraser. Me.

ATWOOD: And you and me. There were six of us.

CALLWOOD: In one number we turned around on our bloomers.

ATWOOD: Yes, that was in the one in which we all had Farley Mowat beards. Being all of Farley Mowat's height, we all looked exactly like Farley Mowat. It was very upsetting actually.

CALLWOOD: That was a funny number. I said, I didn't know this about Peggy Atwood, that she could do this, and someone said you were a camp director.

ATWOOD: Ah, that, too. No, I wasn't a camp director. I was a camp counsellor. Different thing. But before I was a camp counsellor I was a waitress at an all-boys summer camp and I put on an opera there. People are still around who were in that opera. John Sewell, for instance, was part of the corps de ballet.

CALLWOOD: He's the clumsiest man on earth.

ATWOOD: I'd picked the clumsiest. This was a comic opera with a tragic ending. Everybody suicided with forks at the end of it.

CALLWOOD: *(Laughs)* It showed this wonderfully whimsical side of you. Were you part of the plan to make money for the Writers' Union by writing pornography?

ATWOOD: And did I do my part? I did. I wrote a piece called "Across Canada by Pornograph," which started in the Maritimes and went all the way across to the West Coast and had an appropriate style for each piece.

CALLWOOD: We got Marian Engel a Governor General's Award out of that.

ATWOOD: We did. She started writing *Bear* as part of that series and then realized that it was a novel in itself.

CALLWOOD: It seems to me that Alice Munro promised to try to write pornography, too, but she never pulled it off. Poor Alice. Whatever became of her?

ATWOOD: *(Laughs)* Mine wasn't really pornography. I'm afraid it was parody. This is what happened with a lot of the pieces. It turned out that serious writers could not get their tongues out of their cheeks as one would have to —

CALLWOOD: They just couldn't.

ATWOOD: Well, or they didn't want to do it, or something happened. They got quite a few funny pieces but none that were real breathers, as it were.

CALLWOOD: That was one of the few enterprises of yours that really fizzled.

ATWOOD: That wasn't my idea *(laughs)*.

CALLWOOD: Wasn't it?

ATWOOD: No, I participated, but it wasn't my idea.

CALLWOOD: I remember it being hatched in a booth at the Elgin Hotel in Ottawa during a Writers' Union meeting. I couldn't even try to write such a piece. I didn't try. Anyway, we leap from that with a light, springy step to the fact that there is a Margaret Atwood Society, or maybe dozens of them. What do they do in your life? What's happening?

ATWOOD: Well, they publish a newsletter. Now, let us say that they are not the Blue Jays Fan Club. They don't turn up and —

CALLWOOD: There isn't a cheer.

ATWOOD: Not yet, no. They are a society of academics who do research on my work. And they publish a newsletter for themselves in which they exchange pieces of Atwoodian information and news about whose book is coming out, or whose article is coming out. Occasionally they will say that I'm going to appear somewhere, this kind of thing.

CALLWOOD: When they analyze one of your books, do they come upon meanings that you never dreamed of?

ATWOOD: Many *(laughs).*

CALLWOOD: What a surprise! I see your characters — this is a very amateur attempt to join a Margaret Atwood Society — I see many of the people in your books as stumbling through their lives as gamely as possible. Nothing makes very much sense to them, but on they go. That's not the way you go through your life, but that's what I think —

ATWOOD: Oh, I think that's pretty much the way I go through my life *(laughs)*.

CALLWOOD: They go from one event to another, in a decent, well-intentioned way.

ATWOOD: Oh, some of it's high melodrama, June. Come on. Awful things happen to them.

CALLWOOD: Terrible things happen to them. The metaphors have to be pretty clear for me to see them. In *The Edible Woman*, all the food rotted in the refrigerator, rotted with all those colours. It was such a leap of imagination. I will never forget that.

ATWOOD: June?

CALLWOOD: Yes.

ATWOOD: Imagination had nothing to do with it.

CALLWOOD: Your food was rotting?

ATWOOD: Did you ever room with any gathering of young women in your youth?

CALLWOOD: Yes, I did.

ATWOOD: Do you remember what was in the refrigerator?

CALLWOOD: I roomed with nurses.

ATWOOD::   Were they cleaner?

CALLWOOD: Yes.

ATWOOD: Ah, well there you have it *(laughs)*.

CALLWOOD: So the moss on the milk was something that you discovered firsthand?

ATWOOD: Let us say that I went through my "rooming house and my rooming with roomies" period. Things did tend to accumulate in those refrigerators. If you're living with a couple of other people, it's never clear whose job it is to clean out the fridge.

CALLWOOD: Yes. That part I remember, even with the nurses. A poignant aspect of one of your other novels is the child who is persecuted. One child is part of a group of three, which is a dangerous number for little girls. Because an incident in which that child is ostracized takes place in a ravine near Bennington, where you lived, I thought that you might have known something of that pain personally.

ATWOOD: Well, judging from the mail I've received, I would say 90 to 95 percent of little girls know something about this. It's a big subject in England right now. There's been a lot in the papers about the way that groups of children gang up on other children. I used to think that maybe this had all vanished with the coming of the television generation — that instead of being outside burying each other in snowbanks and stringing each other from trees, they were all in watching other people do that on TV. But apparently not, judging from the mail. A certain amount of it just seems to be normal — that is, between the ages of eight and 12, little girls tend to play with other little girls and they tend to act out their power struggles by exclusion: "We're not talking to her this week." Or, "We're going to cut her out." Then if you get a somewhat disturbed child into the mix, it can become more serious than that. Because the child is having a bad time at home, she will transfer that onto the victim of the week, as it were.

CALLWOOD: I don't understand that meanness.

ATWOOD: Well, you may not understand it, but you can certainly observe it.

CALLWOOD: Yes.

ATWOOD: I suppose the kind way of putting it would be that the children are pushing their limits and trying to work out how to arrange their power hierarchies. Let's not pretend that when we become adults this goes away. It goes under the rug or it takes other forms. It's not as crude, but exactly the same kinds of things go on from time to time.

CALLWOOD: A power struggle.

ATWOOD: Yes, and little boys tend to do it differently. They tend to be much more overt about it. The top dog is based on something observable and clear: Johnnie is best at baseball, or Billie is bigger. But with little girls, none of these things necessarily count, so you never know why everybody likes Susie and nobody likes Mary. For that reason, the hierarchies are much more unstable and subject to change practically overnight. We will decide that this week Susie's gotten a little bit too big for her boots, so we're all going to be nice to Mary instead.

CALLWOOD: Does that matrix lead to some kind of wisdom about relationships, because you certainly carry that pain for a long time.

ATWOOD: You would be surprised how many people do. I've had lots of opportunities to observe little girls. I was a camp counsellor, and then I had a child. I've had lots of takes at it, and it is the same thing. It becomes very intense with little girls. It's very important to them what their friends think, whether they are right —

CALLWOOD: Is that a rehearsal, the way adolescent dating is a rehearsal or even the way sequential marriage is a rehearsal —

ATWOOD: I think it is more important to women than it is to men not just to be respected but to be liked, to be approved of. Also their way of handling conflict differs. Rather than confronting somebody and saying, "This is what you're doing that I don't like," they will just cut that person out of their life and not discuss it with them.

CALLWOOD: I wonder if *Cat's Eye*, the book we're talking about, which I completely forgot to mention, renewed for so many people the memories of the same pain. You must have had so much mail about that.

ATWOOD: I had a great deal. Another thing that was true was that for a period in the '70s, we were all supposed to assume that sisterhood was natural and —

CALLWOOD: That women would be nice to one another. I remember that.

ATWOOD: We were all supposed to assume that motherhood was natural in the '50s. Well, in the '70s we were supposed to assume that sisterhood was natural and, therefore, it ought to come to you effortlessly to like all other women and to feel solidarity with them. Consequently, what little girls and women actually did to other little girls and women was not a subject that was discussed.

CALLWOOD: You wanted to clean up your act.

ATWOOD: It was a taboo subject so that it had the air of being brought out from under the rug. A lot of the mail was, "Oh, my goodness! Finally we can talk about this." Or, "I had repressed this. I thought it was just me."

CALLWOOD: The darker side.

ATWOOD: Yes.

CALLWOOD: You brought along another book that is going to help Coach House Press immeasurably, so let's discuss that book. Tell me about it.

ATWOOD: Coach House is also the right publisher for this book. I'm not a total altruist. Don't make me sound nicer than I am *(laughs)*.

CALLWOOD: You're pretty nice. Does that say *Good Bones*?

ATWOOD: *Good Bones*, yes.

CALLWOOD: It's a bit hard to read the type if you don't mind my saying so.

ATWOOD: Well, tell that to the designer. But I don't think so. I think you can see it okay. This is just a mock-up that we're looking at now.

CALLWOOD: I like that person on the cover.

ATWOOD: That is my person. It's my collage. I made it myself. Here we have a leg, and the wings are made of mouths and the tail is eyes.

CALLWOOD: And what is inside this?

ATWOOD: I did a book in the early '80s called *Murder in the Dark*, which was an assemblage of short pieces that were not easy to classify. You couldn't call them poems, you couldn't call them short stories. They were pieces, and *Good Bones* is another book of pieces like that.

CALLWOOD: Like Camus' *Carnets*? Just bits of thought?

ATWOOD: Well, his are more like notebooks of his thoughts. Mine are definite pieces. If I were being very, very trendy, I could call them performance pieces because, in fact, they do do very well in performance. They're short, they're self-contained, and a lot of them are quite funny. For instance, I recommend to you a piece called "Let Us Now Praise Stupid Women."

CALLWOOD: I like it already *(laughs)*.

ATWOOD: I've always been bothered by that scene in *Hamlet* in which he bursts into his mother's dressing room and starts telling her who she can sleep with. So there's a piece called "Gertrude Talks Back." These are a couple of examples, but it's those kinds of pieces.

CALLWOOD: How is the sale of this book going to help Coach House?

ATWOOD: Well, Coach House is a small literary press and, of course, as we know, about 80 percent of the young writers who come into the literary market come in through small literary presses. So they are the doorways. Without those doorways, young writers find it a lot harder to get in. So let us hope that the money generated by the book will help decrease the deficit. All these places have deficits.

CALLWOOD: There's something else I've been wondering about. Someone in Germany was collecting answers to the question,

What is the meaning of life? He said he sent it out to 400 people in Canada.

ATWOOD: Yeah, I got that.

CALLWOOD: What did you say?

ATWOOD: I didn't answer it.

CALLWOOD: Why don't you answer it now?

ATWOOD: Well, because all I would end up doing is telling a very long shaggy dog joke, like the one about the man who sold all his possessions and set out to find out the meaning of life. He crawled through rivers and shredded his clothes and ruined his hands and feet and crawled up a mountain. When he finally got to the guru who was supposed to know the answer, he said, "Great Guru, I have —" and then you go through all the things he's done: he's sold all his possessions, ruined his hands and feet, shredded his clothes, and lost everything he owns, and here he is to find out what is the meaning of life. The guru looks at him and he says, "Life is a fountain." And the man says, "What? You mean I've —" and you go through all the things he's done "— just to have you tell me that life is a fountain?" And the guru says, "So, life isn't a fountain" *(laughs)*.

CALLWOOD: I think that would have been a good contribution.

ATWOOD: That's why Charlie Pachter's huge painting is called *Life Is Not a Fountain*, after that joke. What is the meaning of life? What kind of a question is that?

CALLWOOD: I know, but a lot of people spend their whole lives trying to figure that out.

ATWOOD: Yes, and that's what is the meaning of life for them. What is the meaning of life for me might be quite different from what is the meaning of life for somebody else.

CALLWOOD: People thought with *The Handmaid's Tale* that you were examining the extremes of fundamentalism and that there were some indications that it was a book about un-Christianity, not fundamentalist Christianity, but —

ATWOOD: That's right, yes.

CALLWOOD: While you were doing the book tours and other promotional events the phrase that you kept using is, "All the signs are here." If this book is a non sequitur, it is —

ATWOOD: No, it's not science fiction, by which I mean it's not taking place on the planet Mars, it's not in the future, it doesn't involve technologies that we haven't invented yet. We have all the capabilities for putting a society like this into place.

CALLWOOD: Including the attitudes.

ATWOOD: Especially the attitudes. The clothes I fooled around with, I have to admit. I don't think we're going to get those clothes, based as they are on the Old Dutch Cleanser cans. But everything else is certainly very possible. While I was writing the book, I kept a scrapbook of articles on dictatorships of the past and the present and other pieces of information that fit into my book, because I didn't want anybody saying, "This is just your warped imagination cooking all this up." So I didn't put anything in that hasn't already happened, or isn't happening now, or for which we don't have the technology.

CALLWOOD: Traditionally societies intended to be utopias become catastrophes. So the freedom seems to be an illusion. People will put bars around whatever they can't understand.

ATWOOD: Well, let us put it this way. The 20th-century experience has been that utopias on a grand scale have turned into dystopias, that is, they've turned into their opposite. But unless you have the idea of utopia — that is, the idea that things can become better — you don't try to make any improvements in anything. So it's a paradox.

CALLWOOD: You once said to me that you're an optimist. You then asked with a chuckle if I knew what an optimist was. I said no, falling right into the trap, and you replied that an optimist is someone who's never satisfied.

ATWOOD: Is that what I said?

CALLWOOD: Yes.

ATWOOD: That's not too bad.

CALLWOOD: I didn't think it was too bad, either. In fact, I thought it was pretty good.

ATWOOD: Well, actually, the line I'm pushing these days is that I'm a realist *(laughs)*.

CALLWOOD: What does that mean?

ATWOOD: Well, what it means is that when people say to me, "Why do all these bad things happen in your novels?" I say, "I'm a realist." But I have another reason for why bad things happen in my novels, and that is that if only good things happened in them, they would be terribly boring.

CALLWOOD: *(laughs)*

ATWOOD: Think about it. The first piece in *Good Bones* is called "Bad News." That's what it's about.

CALLWOOD: You just explained that you wrote *The Handmaid's Tale* with clippings right beside you. There is a scene in another book — I can't remember its name — in which two women are in a cell. It felt so —

ATWOOD: *Bodily Harm*, yes.

CALLWOOD: *Bodily Harm*, that's it. It felt like an echo of Amnesty International, which you've supported for years. Did some of that pain come from what you have seen in Amnesty reports?

ATWOOD: Well, I think it's a parallel interest, as it were. In other words, it didn't come from Amnesty. It is, in fact, a very journalistic novel. In that case, it came pretty much from witness accounts. It was based on a real event.

CALLWOOD: There is a kind of precision and carefulness to the way you write and the way you speak. It strikes me that you carry a great sense of order and of what's appropriate into your life. You said that you're now describing yourself as a realist. You have a way of representing the spiritual side of yourself so that it doesn't come out fuzzy.

ATWOOD: Well, among other things, I think we're talking here about a verbal style. There are all kinds of ways of putting words together. Each of them has its own value. For instance, Walt Whitman's was to pile on. Pile on, pile on, pile on more, and if that wasn't enough, to pile on more. So his is a style of excess. Canadians have not habitually gone in for that. They tend to go for a condensed mode of expression, one that's more laconic. That kind of romantic excess and baroque ornamentation is not something you think of as characteristically Canadian.

CALLWOOD: It's the climate. You don't stand up to the cold.

ATWOOD: Someone said to me once, "Why are the lines in your poems so short?" This was when the lines in my poems were short. I said, "Well, it's the winter, you know. You don't want to open your mouth too much because all that cold air gets in."

CALLWOOD: I wasn't talking about style, though. I was talking about style as a way of sometimes masking content, which is probably why people want to go on analyzing your books beyond the point of infinity.

ATWOOD: I don't think it's a masking of the content. I think it's a mode of expression that is literary, by which I mean to say that you don't necessarily name an emotion. You show an emotion. Or you point to an emotion that is around the corner.

CALLWOOD: Your own emotions, though, are closer to the surface than one would gather from the coolness of some of your writing.

ATWOOD: Well, I cry in movies.

CALLWOOD: And when you're hurt, you're really hurt.

ATWOOD: But most people are.

CALLWOOD: Yes, but you haven't developed a very thick skin yet.

ATWOOD: It's thicker than it used to be. I think my rule is more or less this way: Somebody just taking a shot at me, that's one thing. But if they take a shot, for instance, at my researcher or at somebody else involved with me, unfairly, then that makes me angry.

CALLWOOD: You have a sense of justice. You've just described it. But you are also concerned with what's fair for the country, what's fair for an organization. Nothing gets you away from — I was going to say your typewriter, but obviously we're dealing with a pen here — nothing gets you away from your pen faster than your sense that an injustice has been committed.

ATWOOD: Well, again there's a rule. I think that if other people are handling it, then that's fine, they should handle it. When I do get involved, and it's not as often as you might think, it tends to be one of those throw-yourself-in-front-of-the-bulldozer situations. I think it's a question of deciding what is actually going to make any difference. If it's already well under control with lots of very able people, then I don't get involved.

CALLWOOD: What's a conscience? Why are some people moved to altruism, as you are? How does that develop? For a society to survive, you would think it would almost be essential.

ATWOOD: I think it's a human quality, and I think it's more prevalent than we think. We live in a society that tends to somewhat sneer at that quality. We've seen a society — I don't mean Canada, I mean North America or possibly the Western world — in which a great deal of emphasis has been put on competition and on a kind of Darwinian survival of the fittest. If you're rich, then you're the fittest. I think myself that that comes from a misinterpretation of the Bible that took place in the 17th century in Puritan America. There's a verse that says,

"By their fruits, ye shall know them," meaning the just, or the justified. By fruits, of course, I think the Bible probably intended spiritual fruits, but sometime in the 17th century that got interpreted as material fruits. In other words, rich people are better. Rich people are gooder, and poor people are badder. I think that has somehow gotten into the fabric of the society so that they think that way. It's not a medieval way of thinking. Medieval Christianity valued poverty as a spiritual good, which is why the monks were not supposed to own anything.

CALLWOOD: That's interesting.

ATWOOD: But this was a Protestant society, 17th-century Puritan, and they were very interested in that particular verse. We have tended to go on believing in some area of ourselves that if you've got money, you're somehow better. How did I get on to this?

CALLWOOD: I think I was trying to ask in my convoluted way about the development of a conscience.

ATWOOD: Ah, yes. I think that has something to do with the way you were treated as a child. If a child is treated fairly, then the child has a sense of fairness. If a child is not treated fairly, then they really have no model to base that sense of fairness on. So I would put it down to the fact that my brother and I were each allowed two cookies, period. The other interesting thing in our society is that if you start off by saying you're bad, very few people will actually take shots at you, because you've said it. You've said you're bad. So there you are, you're bad. So what are you going to do? Your worst — I'm bad. But if you say that we should be more fair, that we should arrange things better for people or any of these other good things, then there is a reaction against that, which is, who do you think you are — the title of one of Alice Munro's books. Very apt, it's a very Canadian thing, who do you think you are? Just exactly — who do you think you are, telling us where to get off? Telling us how to behave or arrange our society better? So, in fact, you're much more of a target if you try to be good than if you just proclaim your general badness.

CALLWOOD: But without human kindness we would be doomed.

ATWOOD: This is true enough. Therefore, although it's going to put you in a more vulnerable position, you have to keep on. I think we were talking earlier about the necessity of a utopian vision, even though actual utopias have turned into their opposite. Without some idea of this, we're doomed.

Phil Fontaine

$\mathcal{P}$hil Fontaine once spoke at one of those earnest conferences that meet all day in windowless hotel rooms, where people sit on rows of stacking chairs and check their watches a lot. Unlike the other speakers that morning, the Ojibway chief had no notes as he went to the podium. His tone conversational, he addressed the subject of the conference — troubled youth — by talking about his own youth.

I think he may have spoken longer than his allotted time, but who knew? The teenagers in the room, street youth invited out of concern that they should be part of a conference about their lives, were enthralled by him: an articulate, important man whose childhood had been as big a wreck as theirs.

This happened in 1992 in Winnipeg, shortly after Phil Fontaine first had the courage to speak in public of the physical and sexual abuse he suffered in an Indian residential school. Many native children have had the same devastating experience, but few will ever talk of it. His example has enabled others to face their own anguish and begin to heal.

Phil Fontaine was born in 1944 on the Fort Alexander reserve, home of the Sagkeeng Ojibway First Nation and 90 miles north of Winnipeg. He spoke no English until he started school. Twenty years after finishing high school, he graduated from the University of Manitoba with a degree in political science.

He has spent most of his adult life immersed in native politics at every level, from civil servant in the Department of Indian Affairs, as it was known, to grand chief of the Assembly of Manitoba Chiefs.

He was a close runner-up to Ovide Mercredi in 1991 when the latter was elected chief of the Assembly of First Nations.

Phil was a significant figure in the initiative taken by Manitoba chiefs to counter family violence in native life. He says his concern with that issue comes from his personal history of abuse: he understands the patterning of a damaged childhood.

His authority comes from the dignity of his bearing and his piercing-eyed commitment to justice for native people. He is fascinated by aboriginal history and has traced the roots of his people to the time in the 17th century when they were hunters who lived in villages of birchbark domes. Children were safe then. Phil Fontaine wants that for today's native children: a safe childhood.

CALLWOOD: What I'd like to talk to you about first, Phil Fontaine, is an issue that I find very poignant. Native women feel that if there is going to be native self-government that they are going to lose the protection of the Charter [of Rights and Freedoms] and that they'll be victimized by male chiefs, of which you're one. I know that you've answered these questions before and that they are thorny ones, but where do you stand on this issue now?

FONTAINE: Well, there is, of course, some validity to the concerns expressed by our women. I think it's really important that we do all we can to ensure that their interests are advanced and that their rights are protected.

CALLWOOD: Could you give them a guarantee of some kind in your own self-government?

FONTAINE: I think the guarantee that's being accorded First Nations is as much a guarantee for the women as it is for all members of our community. There isn't anyone in our community who will have more rights than another member. That's just the nature of the provisions that are being made for aboriginal people. I think there are enough safeguards.

CALLWOOD: Well, what concerns native women, as it does women of all colours and racial backgrounds, is that most of the people who abuse women and children in families are men.

If the native self-government is in the hands of male chiefs, the women feel that their interests might not be protected. Let me be specific. Wasn't there a case in Manitoba about two years ago where a man granted custody to a father in an abusive situation and ruled against the woman?

FONTAINE: There have been some isolated cases in matters of child custody where the child has been awarded exclusively to a male member of the family. But I think generally it's been pretty balanced. It's true, though, that in many cases of abuse involving children and women the perpetrators have been men. But we're trying to address those issues in Manitoba.

CALLWOOD: What are you doing, because everybody would like to know how to address those issues.

FONTAINE: The first thing that we had to deal with, of course, was domestic violence, violence against women and children. We decided that the best way to do it was to go beyond levelling criticism and to try to come up with answers as to how we address this very complex and sensitive issue. There're no easy answers, there's no magic formula.

CALLWOOD: No, I'm sure there isn't.

FONTAINE: The answer lies within our community, which includes women, men, young people, and elders. So we convened a special assembly, where we brought members of the community of all ages into Winnipeg to talk about the issue of domestic violence. We decided to put our minds together to determine what to do about this very difficult problem. Over 600 people registered, from both First Nation communities outside urban centres and from within urban centres. And we are now working on a five-year strategy plan, which we hope will provide some of the answers that are needed.

CALLWOOD: What were some of the key recommendations to reduce domestic violence?

FONTAINE: Well, one of the big problems that we've inherited is in the area of child welfare. At one time child welfare was the exclusive domain of nonaboriginal governments. It is only —

CALLWOOD: Native children were getting adopted into white families, weren't they?

FONTAINE: Sure. Fifteen thousand kids were adopted out of Indian homes. At least 3,500 of those were from Manitoba and a thousand of those were shipped into the United States. It has only been since 1982 that First Nations communities in Manitoba have had administrative control over child welfare.

CALLWOOD: Wasn't it that very issue, the adoption of native kids, that caused the explosion that led to your getting control of your own well-being as far as children are concerned?

FONTAINE: Well, what we have is administrative control. We don't have jurisdiction. We're mandated by the province. But what we have is something that's far better than what existed prior to 1982, because at least now we have an opportunity to look after our own children.

CALLWOOD: What happens in the classic kind of community where people have felt such despair for generations because of alcoholism and domestic abuse? How can you turn that around?

FONTAINE: One of the things that one has to do is look at the reasons why a certain situation exists, because people have to move beyond blaming themselves for many of the difficulties that they encounter. Many of the problems that we're confronted with are not of our own doing. They have been inflicted on us.

CALLWOOD: I think people accept that that's what indeed happened.

FONTAINE: Recognizing that is the first step to empowering people, and that's what has happened in many regions of the country. People have taken things into their own hands and in the process have empowered themselves. But we still have many steps to take.

CALLWOOD: Where would you start, Phil? Say you're in a village way up in the northern part of the province. Is Flin Flon as far as you can go, or can you go farther than that?

FONTAINE: In Manitoba you can go as far as Churchill.

CALLWOOD: So you're way up north in a small isolated community, where people have been feeling terrible about themselves for a long time. Can one local person turn things around or do outsiders have to come in? How exactly do you go about changing the situation so people have a positive experience instead of a negative one?

FONTAINE: It involves a combination of steps and players. We've learned that we can't rely on outsiders to do things for us. We've learned that the answers lie within our communities. We have to do things for ourselves. We have to be able to control our own destiny. Sometimes it takes one person, sometimes it takes a group to move communities along the path of recovery.

CALLWOOD: Tell us the story of a recovering community, how it healed itself and where it's at. Have you got an example?

FONTAINE: Well, there are many examples. The one that comes to mind, though, is Hollow Water, a community about 140 kilometres northeast of Winnipeg, where the people decided together that they had to do something about abuse against children and women. Fortunately, that community had other examples that it could use. They chose a fly-on-your-own model, which came from Alkali Lake in British Columbia. This community did not deal with the victimizer in the way the justice system had done for far too long, which was to take the victimizer out of the community, put him away for some time, and then bring him back in no better shape and often in worse shape than when he left. Instead these people brought together the victim and the victimizer.

CALLWOOD: Did the family that had been so badly damaged work the problem out on its own or did the whole community work with that family?

FONTAINE: They worked with the entire community. They're still working with the entire community. What they've established is a healing circle.

CALLWOOD: A healing circle?

FONTAINE: Yes, they bring people together. They use elders; they use the strength of the community as opposed to going outside to heal themselves.

CALLWOOD: How do you get a person whose habitual reaction to stress is to hit someone — it's not always a man, but often it is — to change his behaviour?

FONTAINE: It's a matter of education for one thing. You have to get the person to examine why he or she reacts a certain way and then to work on those particular situations. It is one thing to talk about a particular problem that one has, but it's another matter to actually commit oneself to changing.

CALLWOOD: The hardest thing on earth is to change yourself.

FONTAINE: Sometimes it can be pretty scary to look inside oneself because there are many experiences that one holds inside that are shameful, hurtful, and painful. Those experiences are often the very things that cause you to behave in a harmful way towards others.

CALLWOOD: You're acting out the way you feel about yourself.

FONTAINE: You learn to behave the way others have behaved towards you. You learn to do unto others what has been done to you.

CALLWOOD: Sure. The golden rule works both ways, doesn't it?

FONTAINE: Unfortunately it does.

CALLWOOD: Where are you at now that native self-government is being taken much more seriously than ever before in our history? Where is that process at in Manitoba or within the Assembly of First Nations?

FONTAINE: Well, we're very encouraged by all of the events that we've participated in and experienced in the last while. There've been many historic moments in the last two years, and aboriginal people and First Nations people have played a central part in them. That gives us a great deal of optimism for the future.

CALLWOOD: Was Elijah Harper the hinge?

FONTAINE: Elijah Harper is an important figure in all of this. He is a hero in the eyes of many Canadians and for good reason.

CALLWOOD: You were one of the advisors at the time when he vetoed Meech Lake. Were there times when you all wavered and wondered at this course? There was so much criticism and hostility.

FONTAINE: We were convinced that the actions and the steps that we were taking to express ourselves were the right ones. There was considerable pressure, particularly on Elijah, to do it right. And he had some very strong support. The chiefs of Manitoba were very courageous and very committed to doing right for all Canadians, not just for aboriginal people or First Nations people. We didn't want to be excluded. We saw ourselves as an integral part of Canada's future, and we wanted to be part of the decision-making process. We wanted to determine our fate, and what Canada was to become with the rest of the country. Up until that point we had been excluded. So when the opportunity presented itself, we took it and we had a person who was prepared to act on our behalf.

CALLWOOD: Since the process went on for days — not just one historic moment — did Harper appreciate how brave his act was?

FONTAINE: Well, certainly, he understood the enormity of the situation. He felt the pressure, but he was comforted by the fact that many people were very supportive. He saw that he had to take this action in order to secure a future for the people that he represented.

CALLWOOD: For all aboriginal people.

FONTAINE: But, as well, for all Canadians, because we were being forced to live a big lie. We were forced to accept a distortion of history as the truth. Of course, that's not right.

CALLWOOD: That's where the buck stopped, right there with Elijah Harper.

FONTAINE: Absolutely. As one chief in Manitoba described it, the no that was expressed by Elijah was the ultimate act in self-determination.

CALLWOOD: And also the first step.

FONTAINE: The first step we had taken in a long time that demonstrated to all Canadians that what we were saying and what we were doing mattered a great deal.

CALLWOOD: You couldn't have said it more emphatically. I want to change the subject, if I may, and talk a little bit about you. Because my grandparents, especially my grandfathers, were really important to me, I often wonder if that generational influence jumps, if it did in your case. Were your grandparents important?

FONTAINE: They were very important.

CALLWOOD: They're Ojibway on both sides, aren't they?

FONTAINE: Yes, they are. But I lost my grandparents on my father's side when I was quite young. Unfortunately for me and for many others, we lost the very important influence that grandparents might have been able to have on us because we spent a lot of our early days in residential schools.

CALLWOOD: When you were speaking Ojibway and living with your family before you were six, who were the people that you think of as being more important to you?

FONTAINE: My mother for certain. I lost my father during my first year of school when I was seven.

CALLWOOD: How did these people die this young? Your father would have been a young man.

FONTAINE: My father died during an operation. My grandfather on my father's side died when I was four. My grandmother died when I was about 10 years old. But they were still important, because we listened many times to our mother and others talk about what our grandmother did or what our grandfather had been. My grandfather on my father's side was a real character in the community. There were a lot of interesting stories about Charles.

CALLWOOD: Were they hunters?

FONTAINE: Actually, my grandfather delivered mail. I was going to say he was a postman, but he wasn't a postman. He would walk to Selkirk through the bush to pick up mail and deliver mail for the Hudson's Bay.

CALLWOOD: In a Manitoba winter?

FONTAINE: Yes.

CALLWOOD: Oh, my!

FONTAINE: His father, my great grandfather, was a Hudson's Bay servant. He was a steersman on the York boats and looked after an outpost.

CALLWOOD: The Ojibway are boat people, aren't they? They're the ones who ran the canoes for all of the fur trade, weren't they?

FONTAINE: They did many different things. Many of them worked on the York boats and —

CALLWOOD: Tell us what a York boat is. Most people don't know.

FONTAINE: A York boat is one of those big heavy boats. In our case we used them to take furs from Fort Alexander, which was an important post for the Bay, to York Factory. There we traded furs for goods, which we brought back to the south.

CALLWOOD: That was when they were still trading furs for whiskey.

FONTAINE: Well, that was one of the things they did.

CALLWOOD: What do you remember about being an Ojibway kid? What did you know about the Ojibway heritage or traditions?

FONTAINE: Here again it's not necessarily a positive story because we were taken away early. I was six when I entered residential school, and I spent 10 years there so —

CALLWOOD: What are your earliest memories of the times when you were still with your family?

FONTAINE: Oh, I have some wonderful memories actually. On Christmas Eve and New Year's Eve, I recall being bundled up while my father hitched up the team of horses. Then we would go along the frozen river to my grandparents' house, arriving there after midnight. We had to sleep on the floor because there weren't enough beds. The next day we would go to church by sleigh and then visit other relatives.

CALLWOOD: So there wasn't native religion. We're talking about Catholicism, aren't we?

FONTAINE: Yes. The Catholic church had a large influence on us from very early on.

CALLWOOD: Fontaine is French, isn't it?

FONTAINE: Yes it is.

CALLWOOD: So would you be classified as a Métis?

FONTAINE: No, I'm an Ojibway, a status Indian. I was born in Fort Alexander. Actually I was only the second one in my family who was born in a hospital. The rest of the family were born at home with the help of a midwife. One of the better ones in the community was my grandmother, Thérèse.

CALLWOOD: She was a midwife?

FONTAINE: Yes.

CALLWOOD: So she'd go out in the middle of the night. That's when babies are born, you know.

FONTAINE: That's right. She delivered many babies at home.

CALLWOOD: What happened to kids in the residential schools is now an infamous story in our history. Where was the one you were sent to?

FONTAINE: Right in our community. I attended a residential school that was situated three or four miles from home.

CALLWOOD: But cut off from home even though you were that close?

FONTAINE: Very much so. My mother and father attended residential school. It began in 1909. Before that time my grandmother had attended an industrial school in St. Boniface. So all of my brothers and I went to residential school. I'm the 10th boy in a family of 12.

CALLWOOD: Oh, are you, Phil? That's a large family.

FONTAINE: Yes, I have nine brothers and two sisters, and we all went to the residential school. My mother and father had gone before us.

CALLWOOD: Did you all suffer abuse there?

FONTAINE: Oh, I'm certain —

CALLWOOD: You didn't talk to one another about it?

FONTAINE: Well, sure, but we left out many of the more tragic and sad experiences. It was just a way of coping with the shame and the hurt. We suffered a lot of psychological abuse. We were denied our sense of self-worth. We weren't allowed to speak our language. We learned absolutely nothing about our community or our families. We weren't told about the many positive contributions our people had made to the well-being of all people. We knew nothing about the history of our people and much of what we did learn was negative. What we were told, of course, was that to become successful we had to adopt all of the values of the dominant society. Because our school was a Catholic-run residential school what we learned through the history books and what the priests and nuns told us about themselves was a mixture of French and English histories.

CALLWOOD: In which native people didn't figure or figured negatively? Is that what you're saying?

FONTAINE: Yes, we were often portrayed negatively. There was very little positive reinforcement of oneself. So it is not surprising that many of our people, including myself, developed very negative self-images.

CALLWOOD: Did some of you rebel? Were some of you more stubborn?

FONTAINE: Oh, sure. There are always some people who are much stronger than others and those people left.

CALLWOOD: Did they run away?

FONTAINE: Some of them ran away, but others just left very early.

CALLWOOD: What were you like?

FONTAINE: I ran away from school twice. I never got very far, though, and I didn't stay away very long.

CALLWOOD: How old were you when you ran away?

FONTAINE: The first time I was about nine and the second time I was 12. But I didn't make it very far either time, and I ended up back in school.

CALLWOOD: They caught you or somebody turned you in? What happened?

FONTAINE: Yeah, people were concerned about my safety.

CALLWOOD: Did you tell them that you were running away from abuse?

FONTAINE: Oh, no. What drove many of the kids to run away was the sadness that came from being away from family and not liking the environment. Leaving was a way of expressing your sadness. Those of us who ran away understood that we weren't going to get very far, that we were going to end up at home. But at least you'd see your mother, you'd see family, and that was better than we had. At school the only time we could be with family was on Sunday when there was a visit that lasted for two hours. The rest of the time we were in the residential school and we didn't see our parents.

CALLWOOD: I guess the psychological abuse went on underneath the surface for almost everybody. Many also suffered physical abuse, but only a few suffered sexual abuse, and you got it all.

FONTAINE: Well I wouldn't say that I got it all and that I was one of the few who suffered from sexual abuse because that experience was shared by many others, far too many. But certainly all of us suffered psychological abuse, physical abuse, denial, deprivation.

CALLWOOD: Did you try to cope with the sexual abuse by blocking it out as many people do?

FONTAINE: You do what you can to survive, to hide the shame and the hurt. As I mentioned earlier, one of the ways we were able to cope was by laughing about what was happening to us and making light of the bad experiences. The rest of the time you suffer in silence. In some cases, the strong who suffered abuse took it out on the weaker. They learned to perpetuate the abuse inflicted on them.

CALLWOOD: Do you have to deal with those feelings of rage and frustration in yourself?

FONTAINE: Well, if you don't deal with those kinds of feelings, you carry them with you and inflict pain on others. What you have to do, as so many of us are learning to do now, is be able to talk about these experiences.

CALLWOOD: How did you get the courage to talk about them? I'm wondering because I was talking to a Cree man who says that he doesn't think he could ever tell anyone what happened to him. He doesn't know where you got the strength to do that.

FONTAINE: I think I was able to because my wife, Janet, gave me so much support. As well, I felt we needed to talk about the future and to try to decide what was best for us. If you're going to talk about the future, you require some vision. You need clarity of mind, which you won't have if you're burdened. And so you have to be able to let yourself go. In some situations you have to put yourself in the hands of others again.

CALLWOOD: You were trying to be a role model, were you, so that people could talk about it?

FONTAINE: Well, I thought that someone had to take a step to force people to realize that the residential school experience was one that we had to put to rest. But we weren't going to be able to do that unless we talked about what happened in these schools. There were some 87 of these schools run across the country by various religious denominations.

CALLWOOD: What put you on the path of getting a higher education?

FONTAINE: A lot of support from my mother, who pushed me along, and from the rest of my family and others who were very committed to higher education in the community.

CALLWOOD: Did you like learning or were you really pushed into it?

FONTAINE: I didn't particularly enjoy learning what was being taught to us in those schools. I had other interests that were impossible for me to pursue.

CALLWOOD: What were they?

FONTAINE: Well, I like to read. But what we had to read wasn't of much interest to me. We didn't do anything because it was of interest to us, but rather because we were told to do it.

CALLWOOD: Later you became involved in aboriginal politics. How did that happen?

FONTAINE: I wouldn't say it was by design. It was by chance. I was in the right place at the right time. But I also must admit that I've encountered some people who were just outstanding in their field. Politically I had the privilege of being associated with the grand chief of Manitoba, Dave Courchene, Sr., who was there when I was expressing an interest in doing something for the community I'm from. I learned from him as I learned from others. I became chief in 1972 and held the position for four years. Then I joined the federal government, and there again I met someone who has been a mentor to me, a fellow named Cam Mackie, who was an assistant deputy minister in the Department of Indian Affairs. He's been a very strong support throughout the last 15 years.

CALLWOOD: I see a pattern: you work with people, you are a collaborative person. Maybe that's the native style. In the collaborative process of addressing the issues of family violence, you said everybody sat down with the elders. We often hear now that people consult with the elders. Who are elders? How does a person become an elder?

FONTAINE: Well, it's not just someone who's older than the rest of us. I think it's whoever is recognized as having experienced life in different ways and who has become a respected member of a particular community and is seen in some situations as a teacher, in others as a healer. But more generally an elder is someone that you can go to in times of need who can give you some very solid advice because he or she has experienced life and understands life and appreciates it.

CALLWOOD: Is it handed down in families?

FONTAINE: No. It's something that's earned. It's not like being chief. In some situations, chiefs inherited their positions. More often now today they're elected. But elders are those people that have a stature in a community.

CALLWOOD: What Jewish people call a mensch, a person who is a realized person.

FONTAINE: Yes, exactly. If someone has to speak at a gathering, he or she can turn to an elder and this elder will undoubtedly offer him or her some wisdom.

CALLWOOD: What happened to the faith of the people who had such shattering experiences at Catholic residential schools? Did your faith survive these bad experiences?

FONTAINE: Well one must be mindful of this one thing, of course. Because of the shame that results from these experiences, there's a lot of anger and bitterness. I was raised as a Catholic. I went to a Catholic-run residential school, so I was and still am angry with the church for what it did. But I don't want to suggest that the people who run these schools were all out to do harm to us. Many of them meant well and were really committed to the well-being of their charges. But I was very angry, and in recent years I've turned to the traditional teachings for some of the answers that I'm looking for. I've come to realize that there's no need to be exclusively Catholic or Anglican or traditional. One can borrow from each religion to find meaning in one's life.

CALLWOOD: What do you borrow from the Ojibway faith and traditions to find meaning in life?

FONTAINE: The reverence for all living things. Everything that's around is important. No one being is more important than another. And there's no fear in life, you see.

CALLWOOD: No fear?

FONTAINE: Well, it should not represent a fearful experience, in the sense that it's just another step along this long path that we're on to peace and harmony.

CALLWOOD: You don't fear death?

FONTAINE: Myself, I do. That's something that I learned from the teachers of the church and it's something I've had to grapple with for a long time.

CALLWOOD: Does life go on in some form after death?

FONTAINE: Yes, we become part of the spirit world. We're still very much part of what is around us. We just take another form. In some ways it's no different than what you learn from the Christian churches who also teach their —

CALLWOOD: Heaven and hell?

FONTAINE: Well, there's no hell in the Ojibway teachings.

CALLWOOD: In Ojibway you don't use that kind of coercion. What do you use for good behaviour?

FONTAINE: It really comes back to the reverence for life. You look around yourself and thank the Creator for making all things possible and for making the earth in such a way that everyone can make a contribution to its well-being. According to traditional teachings it's Mother Earth that gives life. Women are the life-givers. And the earth sustains you, so you care for it. Land is something that we can never own or possess. We can only care for it. I should make it clear that I haven't come to the stage in my life where I can say, yes, I know and understand the Ojibway teachings, or the traditional teachings. What I have is just a mere glimpse into this vast —

CALLWOOD: Are there Ojibway people who have this wisdom, Phil?

FONTAINE: Oh, sure. There are people who are outstanding teachers and know so much about the Ojibway. Take any First Nations tribal group in this country and you will find people who are immensely knowledgeable about these very important teachings and willing to pass on their knowledge.

CALLWOOD: In the Catholic church the confessional is used as a cleanser, which allows you to rid yourself of things that feel awful. Do the sweat lodges provide a similar outlet?

FONTAINE: There's a difference between the two. In the confessional there's only you and the priest, whereas in the sweat ceremony a group of people come together to support each other, to share with each other, and to pray for others. It's not so much for yourself and you do it in a very trusting way.

CALLWOOD: Is the sweat an ecstatic experience?

FONTAINE: It can be. It depends on what kind of sweat you go to. There are healing sweats, for example. They're all very moving experiences, of course, but they're all different; they're all unique. The important thing in my view is what each person brings to the gathering.

CALLWOOD: The only sweat lodge I've ever seen is inside a prison. There's one in a maximum-security prison near Kingston. It must be a source of hope for native people in prison, where we have a disproportionate number of them, that their faiths are now being recognized.

FONTAINE: One of the ways out of the very difficult situation that too many of our people find themselves in is to go back to the traditional ways and teaching, because they provide hope and a means of bringing people together. They can empower people. And in our situation we need to empower ourselves.

CALLWOOD: In Freudian terms, or psychoanalytical terms, you go back to your roots in order to regrow yourself in a better way.

FONTAINE: What the traditional teachings and ways offer you is respect for yourself. They give you pride and dignity, which have been missing in the lives of many native people. We need to be comforted with the thought that we are as important as the next person and that we have something to offer.

CALLWOOD: As you know, the general public throughout the country is much more supportive of aboriginal rights than ever before in our history. I think the change in attitude can be attributed to the dignity of the native leaders. All of you men and women are showing such composure that you're winning a public relations fight. That's a crass expression to use, but that's what it is. The message that you're being reasonable and strong is a very powerful one.

FONTAINE: I think people recognize that there's a great deal of substance to many of the outstanding aboriginal leaders they have come to know. These leaders have contributed to the important process of educating and informing people. If we're going to continue to reach out to people for support, it's incumbent upon us to educate and inform them. It's an important process in the changes that we are asking for. And it's far better to bring about change through negotiation rather than confrontation, even though the latter method often forces the government to respond more quickly.

CALLWOOD: But sometimes there's a whiplash, too.

FONTAINE: That's right. And since the process of change that we're engaged in is a long one, it's far better to reach out to people and to bring about change willingly as opposed to having people resist it. Still, it's important to realize all the while that people are resistant to change.

CALLWOOD: Yes, people hate change. Where are you on your own path, Phil? Are you feeling good about yourself?

FONTAINE: What I'm engaged in now is a healing process. I'm on a path of self-discovery and I've just begun.

Rosemary Brown

Speaking of the women's movement, Rosemary Brown once uttered the memorable line: "Unless all of us have made it, none of us has made it." When I interviewed her for *National Treasures*, she was between careers, something that happens in her lifetime with tidal regularity, and she was wondering with sunny equanimity what would turn up next. As it turned out, her next career was to head Ontario's Human Rights Commission, a perfect spot for this levelheaded, wise woman.

The job she had just left was executive director of MATCH International Centre, which gives support to women in Third World countries, and she was proud of what MATCH has accomplished. Rosemary's other activities give some sense of her versatility, intelligence, and dedication to justice. For instance, she was for 14 years a member of the British Columbia Legislature, retiring in 1986; she was chair of women's studies at Simon Fraser University and taught social work at the University of British Columbia; she was the first woman to run for leadership of a national party (the New Democratic Party in 1975); she was one of the founders of the Vancouver Status of Women Council; she wrote a book about her political life she titled, *Being Brown*.

She is also a rivetting orator. More than a thousand women turned out in a Toronto hotel one morning at seven-thirty to have breakfast and hear her speak at a benefit for LEAF, an organization that funds legal battles for women's rights. Rosemary, beautifully dressed and serene, had just come from Vancouver, so for her it was four-thirty in the morning, but her speech was passionate, funny, and eloquent. She got *two* standing ovations.

She was born in Jamaica and after her father's death she was raised in what she calls "a woman's house" by her well-to-do mother and grandmother. Confident and outgoing, she came to Canada in 1950 to attend university and encountered racism for the first time in her life. Shocked, she decided to leave Canada but instead fell in love. She married William Brown, who was to become a doctor, obtained a graduate degree, and launched herself as a social worker while raising three children. The family moved to Vancouver and she settled herself in the NDP, where she figured she had the best shot at combatting racism and sexism. Besides, her grandmother was a social democrat and Rosemary was raised to believe that politicians could change the world. Her grandmother used to say that the right to vote was worth dying for.

Within three weeks of her appointment as chief commissioner of the Ontario Human Rights Commission, Rosemary Brown was hotly attacked for something in a report prepared before her arrival. In an interview with Lynda Hurst of the *Toronto Star*, she was laconic. "I thought, well, at least I'd get a month. . . ." she shrugged.

CALLWOOD: Rosemary, 16 years ago you came within a hair-breadth of being the leader of the federal NDP. However, the male establishment ganged up on you. I want to take you back to that defeat because it now seems extraordinary that David Lewis could have said you were a dangerous woman to the party.

BROWN: Yes.

CALLWOOD: What was behind that, Rosemary?

BROWN: Well, I've had some time to think about it. In retrospect I believe he was probably quite right, because, in fact, I certainly did represent some major changes in direction. I was running for the leadership at a time when women were becoming more actively involved not just in politics but in taking control of their lives and the situations that had made their condition the way it was. It is quite possible that in trying to change the direction of the party to take this into account, as well as to take into account our relationship with ethnic and racial minority groups, that I could have changed the party in very profound ways. Maybe those were not the ways in which David Lewis would have liked to see the party go at that time.

CALLWOOD: You were prophetic, though, weren't you?

BROWN: Well, in some respects, but you know David was, too, in a lot of ways. He was a good person who worked really hard and built the party, as you know. It's very difficult to deal with a different vision when you've held one of your own for so long. Certainly women were not part of the original equation.

CALLWOOD: I was disappointed to see that Tommy Douglas also felt that you shouldn't be leader. That seemed out of character to me.

BROWN: Yeah, but today they would have been different.

CALLWOOD: Oh, yes, that was then, but just imagine not only were you a woman but a black woman.

BROWN: Yeah.

CALLWOOD: What a thing it was that you came so close.

BROWN: Amazing, isn't it, for a country that is not very tolerant of either women or blacks?

CALLWOOD: At what point did you know you were going to lose? How did that happen?

BROWN: I guess it was on the final ballot when one of my workers came over and said that in order to beat it I would need to have at least two thirds of the Saskatchewan vote. Saskatchewan, as you know, has never even elected a woman from the NDP to their provincial house or their federal house, so the idea of two thirds of the Saskatchewan delegates supporting me was just fantasy.

CALLWOOD: You have to go on smiling, do you?

BROWN: Yes.

CALLWOOD: I remember Flora MacDonald when she lost, in similar circumstances. There was a gang-up of Progressive Conservatives against her that time so that she was obliged to walk across the floor and make it unanimous. She did it with great grace. Did you have to do that, too?

BROWN: Yes. But then I wanted to make it unanimous. I think that the most divisive thing that can happen to a political party is a leadership race. There are a lot of wounds that have to be healed when that is over, and the sooner you can get started on the healing process the better. So I certainly wanted to make it unanimous and to make it absolutely clear to the nearly 43 percent of the delegates there who supported me that I wanted them to start supporting Ed.

CALLWOOD: In view of the fact that Ed entered the race because they wanted him to beat you, that was very generous of you, I think.

BROWN: Well, no Ed was actually quite wonderful the whole way through the campaign. We disagreed on the fact that he thought he would have been a better leader than I. But other than that one basic disagreement we got along very well. He was always very courteous and thoughtful.

CALLWOOD: Your nomination speech was a barn burner, and it was about children. Wasn't that the time that the National Council on Welfare had that *Poor Kids* report?

BROWN: Yes, and I think the most depressing thing about that report is that if they were to release a similar one today, the statistics would be exactly the same.

CALLWOOD: Rosemary, you're dead-on. They have done a second report. I don't think it's called *Poor Kids*, but the figures are still the same. There are over a million children living in poverty.

BROWN: One in six.

CALLWOOD: And what are the consequences that you've seen yourself as a social worker and a politician?

BROWN: Well, to me it's criminal. I mean, if this were a really impoverished country, one could be sympathetic towards those statistics, but it isn't. It is supposed to be one of the richest countries in the world. We have one of the highest standards of living, yet that we would tolerate —

CALLWOOD: Children in food banks.

BROWN: Children in poverty is absolutely incomprehensible.

CALLWOOD: How did you ever get the nomination in the riding of —

BROWN: Vancouver-Burrard.

CALLWOOD: Vancouver, no Burnaby —

BROWN: Vancouver-Burrard was my first one.

CALLWOOD: How did you get that nomination?

BROWN: Well, it was a miracle. But like the story of so many things in my life, it came out of the hard work of women and the support of women, because women certainly were responsible for my entry into politics and for the success that I enjoyed there.

CALLWOOD: That was when? Was that in the '60s some time?

BROWN: That was 1971 because I won that nomination —

CALLWOOD: Dave Barrett was head of the party at the time.

BROWN: Yes.

CALLWOOD: You won the election, as well. How did you do that?

BROWN: Well, it was a miracle for the NDP really, and it was certainly a miracle for me and for Emery Barnes. We were the two black candidates. It was just incomprehensible to me that I would be representing a riding in which it was so difficult for me to get housing and almost impossible to find a job. I thought, you know, Canadians are crazy. I mean they really are a little bit mad. They don't want you to live in their house or next door to them. They don't want you to work for them, but they'll elect you to go and represent them. That touch of madness is something that has always fascinated me about racism in this country.

CALLWOOD: David Barrett was something of a disappointment to a lot of us on women's issues when he was premier.

BROWN: That was his Achilles heel, because in every other respect he was so forward thinking and positive. The women's movement really shook up that generation of men. They were totally unprepared for it, and so they all behaved badly. None of them would sit down and be rational about it. The immediate response was to be defensive and say no, it can't happen. It was very disappointing to all women of my generation that they responded that way.

CALLWOOD: That's when women first started marching out. Do you remember Michael Snow's *Walking Woman*?

BROWN: That's right.

CALLWOOD: That's when women started to move. I've been asked to run, and I've always thought what a sacrifice of your family life it is for a woman to go into politics. I guess you're a very good example of the cost, aren't you?

BROWN: Well, I think it's as Heather Robertson said in her recent book on political wives, that as more women become elected and we see more spouses of politicians being male, we'll realize just how ludicrous the role of the woman really is in this situation, because, in fact, husbands do not behave like political wives. They really don't. When a woman goes into politics, she's taking on an additional job, because husbands don't drop everything that they're doing to support you. The best that you can ask is that they decrease the demands that they make on you. If you can negotiate that with them, then you're ahead of the game. But I was very lucky in a number of ways. Because Bill has a profession of his own and is very independent and strong in his own field, I didn't have to worry about bruising his ego, although there were other people who were concerned about that. The other thing is that he was such a good and caring parent that I didn't worry about the fact that from Monday to Friday he was in charge of our three children. I knew that they would be well cared for, so that made my task a lot easier.

CALLWOOD: Some of the women who've done well in politics are women who have no family. Barbara McDougall springs to mind, as do Flora MacDonald, Judy LaMarsh, and Pat Carney. It nearly caved Pat Carney in to commute, didn't it?

BROWN: Well, I think until my time, just about all of the women in the federal house were either unmarried, childless, or their children were adults. The idea of federal politicians having young babies, like Sheila Copps and others, is totally new. It just didn't happen during the time of Ellen Fairclough and Grace MacInnis.

CALLWOOD: Grace died just a little while ago. What a career she had — the only woman in the House of Commons for years!

BROWN: She was absolutely amazing, and that must have been a really lonely place to be, especially raising the issues that she did around choice. Imagine the courage that must have taken in those days, the courage that it takes today.

CALLWOOD: She and I once had a debate about whether you could have more influence on change outside government or inside. She held for inside and I for outside. We decided to call it a draw. How would you call it?

BROWN: Well, I think we need both. The politician is only as strong as the outside pressure, and the outside pressure is only implemented when you have women inside who can actually push to get the caucus and the cabinet to do it. We need both. I can't see us using either one or the other in isolation.

CALLWOOD: I wonder if your being not just the first woman in politics in many places but also being a black woman made it a little different, a little easier in a funny way. Already you're exotic because you're black. You even have an accent that marks you as unique. Does that mean you could be seen not as a pathfinder but as one of a kind, as someone not so threatening?

BROWN: I'm not sure I would say not quite so threatening. It's a two-edged sword. Part of it is that every black woman is assumed to be Rosemary Brown. In fact, all of my friends at one time or another have been mistaken for me, because, the assumption is that if you are black and you're female and you're a certain age, you must be Rosemary Brown so that makes —

CALLWOOD: A lot of you out there.

BROWN: A lot of us are out there. The other thing is that I'm exotic only to the people who support what I'm doing. To the people who are opposed to it, I'm very threatening. They see me as being very dangerous and very evil in a lot of ways. I write a column for a newspaper in Vancouver and even now I still get the kind of mail that really is quite scary because it depicts me as being this very powerful, dangerous person who bears no relationship to the Rosemary Brown I have to live with.

CALLWOOD: That's paranoia, isn't it?

BROWN: It's really amazing, so I think the perception is it depends. The other thing, too, is in a lot of ways I think I get Canada off the hook. It's very difficult to accuse a country of being racist when they can say, Well, good heavens, we have Lincoln Alexander, we have Rosemary Brown, Howard McCurdy, Emery Barnes. So they're off the hook, and that's really not what it's all about. What it's all about is that you know the discrimination and the prejudice exists.

CALLWOOD: What's worse, sexism or racism?

BROWN: Again, I cannot separate them. They're both sides of the same coin. I think that if you happen to be both black and female, you carry both of them. In a lot of ways you learn from each experience. When I came to fight sexism as a black person, I found that I was better prepared because I'd been through the experience in terms of my human rights. But if I had to choose between one or the other, I wouldn't take either.

CALLWOOD: Democrat Shirley Chisolm, who was a potential candidate for the United States presidency, said that she thought the greater disadvantage was being black.

BROWN: Yes, well, the United States is different. Their experience and history of racism is quite different from ours.

CALLWOOD: More overt.

BROWN: Yes, it certainly has been more overt, and it seems to be older, it has been around longer. So based on her experience, that's quite possible. I find that even after you've dealt with racism, even within the context of a community in which you are treated equally because you're black, you still run into sexism. So you never get away from it.

CALLWOOD: And black men aren't very receptive to the women's movement.

BROWN: No, they're not. They're trying, as all men are, but it's a revolution, you know. It's challenging.

CALLWOOD: It really is a revolution. Let's go back in time for a minute. When I read about your childhood in your book, *Being Brown*, it seemed idyllic. You were raised with a wonderful sense of freedom and privacy and love.

BROWN: It was wonderful and I really long for the Jamaica of those years, but it's gone, of course. However, I consider myself very lucky to have had that childhood.

CALLWOOD: You are the child of that childhood, aren't you?

BROWN: Yes, very much so.

CALLWOOD: Tell me about the women, the strong women, around you.

BROWN: Well it's amazing when you look back on it. The men in my family all died when they were quite young and so that left a grandmother. I have almost no memory of my grandfather at all. I think he actually died before I was born, but my grandmother is certainly the woman in our family whom I remember most vividly and then my aunts and my mother. The only man in our family was one uncle, and he was never treated as though he was a powerful, controlling figure. He was just one of the family. The people who made the decisions around me were always women. I grew up in my grandmother's house, and it was a house that was filled with women and children.

CALLWOOD: I liked the part where I could see that there was a place for you to live in your imagination. Most children have no room anymore. There's no privacy for a child. But you could escape in any direction it seems.

BROWN: Yes, it was quite wonderful. In retrospect I realize that it was a gift.

CALLWOOD: And you developed the ability to give speeches in your childhood. That's a hoot, the idea of you giving these speeches to yourself.

BROWN: Yes, I always had this fantasy that I was going to be a courtroom lawyer who was going to be so brilliant that, of course, I'd win all of my cases, not with logic or anything but just rhetoric. It was wonderful. Young people often say to me, when I speak at high schools, "How did you learn to speak like that?" It's almost as though you have to start that early to develop the confidence to do it. It's not as though you can take a course in later life, because you never seem to be as comfortable when you're speaking then as you do when you have done it all of your life. I've listened to people in other professions talk about when they first decided they wanted to be a musician or a dancer or whatever, and it always goes back to their childhood.

CALLWOOD: Well, you were saturated in politics, weren't you?

BROWN: Yes, I never developed a knack for small talk until I started going to cocktail parties.

CALLWOOD: You talked politics when you were a little kid in your family.

BROWN: Oh, yes. We had very serious discussions.

CALLWOOD: Jamaican politics is pretty serious stuff.

BROWN: Absolutely, and so is colonial politics, not just in terms of the Caribbean but also in terms of what England was doing with the colonies. The grown-ups always expected us to listen when they were having these adult conversations and they expected us to ask questions. They took the time to explain the issues in detail so that we could understand them. Consequently, we had a very clear understanding of politics all of our way through life.

CALLWOOD: Is that where you developed a sympathy for what would be called left-wing politics?

BROWN: Oh, yes. I don't think that it came out of any sort of ideological commitment so much as out of a sense that something was wrong and the only way to set it right was to have these kinds of principles and attitudes towards it. Later on in life a name was affixed to this way of thinking. But I don't think my grandmother ever would have referred to herself as a social democrat. She just knew that you just didn't do things that way.

CALLWOOD: Was that as a result of her religious upbringing or was she working it out on some other principles?

BROWN: I think it was based primarily on her Christianity, on her belief that certain things were morally acceptable and certain things weren't.

CALLWOOD: Are you what we would call a Christian?

BROWN: I would say that my social commitment is certainly rooted in my Christian upbringing. But I don't translate the Bible literally. I don't do something this way instead of that because the Bible says to. Rather, because I grew up having to go to church three times on Sundays, having to learn all of these quotations from the Bible, and having to participate in family worship every single evening, a sense of morality inevitably became part of my life. So by the time ethics changed and we became a generation that would do whatever made you feel good, it was too late for me. I already knew when I was doing right and when I was doing wrong.

CALLWOOD: Are you hard on yourself when you think you've done wrong?

BROWN: Well, I try not to do wrong, because I am very hard on myself. I have spent a lot of my life wrestling with principles and certainly the ethical issues that we have to confront today didn't exist when I was young.

CALLWOOD: Whatever happened to black and white? There's a justification for every side of an argument.

BROWN: Right and you really have to wrestle today with those issues. I think that part of the reason why society just says do what makes you feel good is that there's an incipient laziness. People don't want to confront those kinds of issues and see how they measure up with their understanding of what is acceptable and what isn't.

CALLWOOD: It is hard work.

BROWN: It is incredible. I mean the idea of surrogate motherhood would have been considered impossible in the past.

CALLWOOD: I know.

BROWN: Who ever heard of babies being born in test tubes or —

CALLWOOD: Let me tell you about a recent development that poses a moral dilemma for me. A very poor teenager wanted to have an abortion. However, she was persuaded by her doctor to have her baby instead and to sell the baby for $10,000, which she did. The couple who bought it liked it so much that they asked her to have another one for them. Now she suddenly has a new profession. She has money. It's her body. Look at all those arguments and yet everything in me says that's terribly wrong.

BROWN: Absolutely unheard of.

CALLWOOD: Those are dilemmas that we all have now.

BROWN: And I have a sense that they're going to become more difficult. Now that we have frozen eggs how do you decide whether a child should live or die? What eggs should be saved and which ones should be flushed down the toilet? Are we going to start breeding a master race? How do we protect ourselves from making bad decisions about issues like these?

CALLWOOD: A commission has been created to address some of these questions, hasn't it?

BROWN: Yes, but I'm afraid the ramifications are too wide-ranging to be dealt with by a commission. And we don't need a commission on birth technologies, we need a commission on ethics.

CALLWOOD: They cross over right there. That's an intersection.

BROWN: Yes.

CALLWOOD: You reach so many people because of your ability to give speeches. Do you still work as hard on them? I once heard that you rehearsed over and over again. Do you still do that?

BROWN: Well, let me confess first that I really hate giving speeches.

CALLWOOD: Do you?

BROWN: Oh, I still become so stressed and nervous after all of these years. I do prepare. I do a lot of reading. I'm a voracious consumer of information because I want to always have my information up to date. Then I have to wrestle with that information and distill it before presenting it so that I'm coming from a point of view that is positive and helpful rather than destructive. I always worry about whether what I say is the correct thing to be saying at this time and under these circumstances.

CALLWOOD: You never seem to be reading. You look up more than you look down.

BROWN: Yes, but a speech is written in my head over a period of about two weeks. Then it goes through at least four drafts on my computer. It's a full-time job giving a speech. So I never just talk off the top of my head.

CALLWOOD: You don't?

BROWN: No, I never do that.

CALLWOOD: You wouldn't take a chance?

BROWN: Well, I will, but you can be sure that what comes out is not off the top of my head. Because you influence people by the things that you say, you have to be very careful that they're thoughtful and constructive.

CALLWOOD: You once engaged in a filibuster in the B.C. legislature?

BROWN: Yes.

CALLWOOD: What was that all about and how did you do it?

BROWN: I was trying to stop the dismantling of what we called resource boards, which was a process whereby we allowed communities to make decisions about the social services in their communities. Instead of the Province of Ontario making all the decisions about social services for the province, we allowed communities to elect their boards. Because you are making decisions for your community, you know everybody in your community. You know exactly what their needs are, and you are responsible for disbursing funds. Well, of course, there was a change of government and the new government wanted to centralize everything in Victoria again and all decisions had to be made there and so in an attempt to forestall the passing of this bill, I engaged in a filibuster.

CALLWOOD: How long did you speak for?

BROWN: I think it was just over 15 hours.

CALLWOOD: That's amazing. I also found it very poignant that you didn't know anything about racism until you went to Montreal to attend McGill University. Wouldn't that be a shock . . .

BROWN: Well, I certainly had never experienced it at that level.

CALLWOOD: You couldn't get a roommate?

BROWN: No. Did you know that McGill gave me an honorary degree last summer? I was really quite touched by that and —

CALLWOOD: What did you say? Did you give the convocation address?

BROWN: Yes, I did. When he was introducing me, the vice-chancellor talked about my experiences at McGill.

CALLWOOD: Did he talk about racism?

BROWN: Yes, so it wasn't necessary for me to dwell on that.

CALLWOOD: Oh, Rosemary, you have a lot of doctorates. What do you tell students?

BROWN: Well, in this day and age when this country seems to be hell-bent on blowing itself apart, I concentrate on talking to students about putting the constitutional debate into perspective. I suggest that they closely examine the decisions they make in this regard. I ask them to reflect upon what will happen to Canada as a result of whether they decide to support the Constitution, amend it, or defeat it. I also suggest that they look at the situation not just in terms of their own personal experience but that they try to look at this country as the home of a number of different people of different cultures and races, different languages, different experiences. I also tell them to look at the role that Canada plays in the world at large. We have a very clear place, which we don't want to jeopardize.

CALLWOOD: I'm amazed that you stayed here. You must have been tempted so many times to go back to that idyllic island of yours.

BROWN: I still am, but as I say my Jamaica lives in my head. It really is not there anymore.

CALLWOOD: But didn't you think of returning when you were first at McGill and you were crushed by the things that were happening to you?

BROWN: Oh, yes. I was quite prepared to leave immediately, but you know what happened. It's the story of every woman's life.

CALLWOOD: No, what happened?

BROWN: Well, that's where I met Bill, and as I like to tell this story, he promised that if I married him he would make me happy for the rest of my life.

CALLWOOD: How did that work out?

BROWN: We'd live happily ever after. I often say to him, "I kept my end of the bargain." Since he was from the United States studying in Canada, this was not his home either, and we both agreed that this is where we'd like to live.

CALLWOOD: Did he find the racism in Montreal different from American racism or was he more prepared?

BROWN: He actually came to Canada to get away from racism in the South. He's from Georgia, so he found Canadian racism more polite than American racism. It was easier to experience. But it's interesting that once we had children, it was just as painful. It's so difficult to deal with your children's hurt, isn't it? I mean when someone hurts your child, it's much more painful than when someone hurts you.

CALLWOOD: Would your oldest child have been the only black child in the school?

BROWN: Yes, she was the first one until her brother arrived two years later.

CALLWOOD: What do you think that did to her?

BROWN: It's hard to tell. She appears to be very normal and well-adjusted. We're hoping that she is because what we tried to do was be very supportive and reinforce her own self-esteem. We worked really hard at that when both children were growing up. She and her brother are just two years apart, although years later we had another son. Right now she's fine. She practises law in Vancouver. She's actually just completed a year at the London School of Economics, where she did her master's in law, and she seems to be incredibly normal.

CALLWOOD: You believe, don't you, that if you make your child as emotionally strong as you can that they'll be better prepared to meet life's challenges?

BROWN: Absolutely. I think that is really crucial. I also think that it is important that your children know what your values are, that they should have a clear understanding of your principles and your sense of integrity. So we were not very trendy parents, I'm afraid.

CALLWOOD: Neither were we. I want to go back to your book for a minute. *Being Brown* was dedicated to women who are struggling for social justice, or something to that effect. The wording was very good. After all the years you've spent in that vineyard, where do you think we're getting?

BROWN: We're moving forward but not as fast as we would like because so many of the gains that we made are being eroded. That happens whenever we become less vigilant about things and start to take them for granted. That said, I don't think we can ever be turned back now, because it's not just us but also our children and their children that now know that there is a different way for women to be treated and for women to live.

CALLWOOD: I don't think we've done much yet for women who are living in poverty, though.

BROWN: That is going to be the toughest one, and unfortunately that's where most women are. But the fact that it's even on the agenda is a major breakthrough.

CALLWOOD: It's a slippery agenda, though. Look how fast day-care came off.

BROWN: That's the danger of not being vigilant. I'm a firm believer in being vigilant. I also think we have to do a better job in our social analysis. We tend to look at symptoms without understanding the underpinnings. We need to ask why these issues are not on the national agenda. Why is it that they are not a priority? Why is it that we tolerate child poverty?

CALLWOOD: It's not just as simple as saying, let's elect more women, or sometimes we don't get the women we want.

BROWN: No, that's where some kind of analysis has to come in, because I believe that it is quite possible for committed men to change things. Why do they not have the commitment? We have to examine that, too. Rather than fighting against issues that concern women, why don't they look at the questions women are raising and see how they can change themselves in order to address some of those problems?

CALLWOOD: When you left politics, you taught women's studies for a while at Simon Fraser. What's the climate like on campus these days? Are young women excited or sceptical?

BROWN: Most of the women in the course were older women. There were some younger women, and one of the hilarious things about the women's studies entry level course at Simon Fraser is that it was very popular with the football team.

CALLWOOD: Oh, come on —

BROWN: Because they thought it was a cinch, you see. There would be women of all ages in the course, but sitting in the back row, looking quite huge and very bored, would be these massive males from the football team. After the first exam, they discovered to their horror that women's studies was not a cinch. They realized that they either had to buckle down and start paying attention or else they would fail the course. However, the women enjoyed the course because a lot of them came with their own experiences, and that's what made the course different. It wasn't simply someone standing in the front and teaching. It was based primarily on an exchange of experiences and then an analysis of those experiences to understand why they happened.

CALLWOOD: When people see that they share certain experiences it can be almost euphoric, can't it?

BROWN: Yes it was very exciting.

CALLWOOD: When you left Simon Fraser, you went to MATCH something.

BROWN: MATCH International.

CALLWOOD: What's MATCH International? I phoned you one time in Ottawa and I'd never heard of this.

BROWN: I'm always amazed by the ideas people have when they hear a name like MATCH International. It is simply an NGO, a non government organization, like UNICEF, which works with women in the Third World and women in Canada. It sets up a symbiotic relationship between Canadian women and women in the poorer countries to the south.

CALLWOOD: Can you give me a specific example?

BROWN: We work on three major issues. One is violence against women, which is not a uniquely Canadian phenomenon. Anywhere in the world where you have women and men, violence is present. The way of trying to eradicate it varies from culture to culture, but what we find almost everywhere is that it is the women who want it to end. They are the ones who develop projects or programs to try to end it. And they're the ones who need the funding because, as you said earlier, they are the ones who are poor. At MATCH we try to raise money to send overseas to help these women with these programs; or we establish an exchange of ideas between the Canadian women who are working against violence and women doing so in other parts of the world; or we facilitate the exchange of resources. There is a kit, for example, that we have developed that looks at violence from an international perspective and offers some techniques for addressing it, politically, socially, economically, educationally. So we work at a number of different levels.

The name MATCH actually came from the founder Norma Walmsley, who started out with the idea of matching Canadian women and women in the Third World, as it was called then. The idea resulted from her experience at an International Women's Year conference in Mexico City, where the women from the south lit into the North American women and said, "Don't speak to us about feminism and sisterhood being global because you are fighting your own struggle. You really do not care about us, because if you did, you would try to help us in our struggle, too."

CALLWOOD: Why do you think men haven't resented the bad image that they get when women say they can't go out in the streets alone at night or can't go into a parking garage at night? That doesn't seem to me a women's problem. That should be a man's problem. Why haven't men done something about it?

BROWN: I think men resent the bad image, but different men respond to it in different ways. Some men become very defensive and say, "Well, if she didn't have on such a tight skirt . . ." or "If she wasn't in such a short dress . . ." or "If she wasn't asking for it, it wouldn't happen." That includes a number of judges who sit in our courts, of course. Other men are trying to do something about it. There are now groups of men in North America working against violence against women.

CALLWOOD: You had no violence in your childhood. I didn't in mine. It's almost incomprehensible to me.

BROWN: I think that to a large extent the absence of violence in my childhood had to do with the fact that I grew up in a women's community. As I said, in my grandmother's house it was primarily women. One of the things that Bill has often said to me is that because I grew up in an environment of women, I never learned to be afraid of men. Nor did I particularly learn to respect them because they weren't there. Consequently, I tend to rush in and treat men as equal, whereas other women will treat them with deference. I never learned how to treat men with deference because I never had to.

CALLWOOD: Women sometimes get a parallel system: one is their family, and the other is their friendships with women, which become another very positive family, so to speak. That seems to have happened to you, too.

BROWN: Oh, yes, there has always been a very strong network

of women in my life and I've always been part of other women's networks. It's been a very rich and rewarding experience.

CALLWOOD: I don't know if very many men can share tears, but women don't have a problem with that.

BROWN: We share laughter, too, which is good — healthy laughter, not hostile laughter.

CALLWOOD: What were the happiest times of your life?

BROWN: I think I'm living through them now. It seems to me that every day brings its own joys and its own sorrows. I loved having children and I was thrilled when I had grandchildren. They are so wonderful, grandchildren. When Audrey became the leader of the New Democratic Party, I thought I would burst with excitement and joy because we had a woman leader. Every day good things seem to be happening.

CALLWOOD: Why did you leave MATCH?

BROWN: Well, I went there for a specific purpose, and that was to raise the profile of the organization and to put it on a firm financial base. Then I planned to retire once again.

CALLWOOD: You're retired again?

BROWN: Oh, yes. This is my third retirement. I love retiring.

CALLWOOD: How long do they last?

BROWN: Well, I never seem to have much control over my retirements. There are still some things I have to learn about. However, one day I want to lead a life of idleness and sloth just to see what it's like, because all my life I was warned against it. My grandmother was a great one for saying, "Do something. Be useful. We can't have you leading a life of idleness and sloth."

CALLWOOD: I'm sure people tell you it will last about 20 minutes. Then you will dust your hands and say, "That's enough idleness and sloth."

BROWN: I suspect that deep down inside there is someone who would enjoy idleness and sloth if I gave her a chance.

CALLWOOD: Well, you've just started your 60s. You've got loads of years of being productive ahead of you if you want to work. Where do you think you're going to go next?

BROWN: I'm doing a lot of writing and speaking. I'm still with MATCH. I've been named a special ambassador, so I'm still raising money for the organization and talking about it. I want to do some of the things I haven't had a chance to do, like more gardening, more listening to opera, more playing with my grandchildren, more just enjoying life.

CALLWOOD: But your grandchildren are scattered all over the place, aren't they?

BROWN: Yes, so the time that I have to spend with them is really very precious.

CALLWOOD: A daughter-in-law of yours is a Cree. So two of your grandchildren are really natives then, aren't they?

BROWN: Yes, they're registered.

CALLWOOD: Has that made you keener on the issues around aboriginal rights?

BROWN: I was involved in that long before. I always identified with the struggle of the native people in Canada because I saw their experience as being very similar to the way in which the Caribbean and the West Indies were colonized by Britain. So the arrival of my grandchildren didn't heighten my interest in native issues. It is amazing, though, to see them talking about their rights at the ages of seven and four.

CALLWOOD: They're talking about their rights?

BROWN: Yes, they understand what is going on because they're growing up in an environment where they're hearing the adults talk about it and they're listening. My seven-year-old grandchild will bring me up to date occasionally about what's happening. It's wonderful.

CALLWOOD: There are parallels with the black movement. There almost had to be a middle class.

BROWN: Yes, there had to be thinkers and professionals and educated people to deal with the convoluted laws that white Anglo-Saxon male society builds around itself to protect itself.

CALLWOOD: To make bridges.

BROWN: Yes, but they're there now and they're going to take care of business.

CALLWOOD: Do you think they're going the right way?

BROWN: Yes.

CALLWOOD: Are women going the right way?

BROWN: Yes.

CALLWOOD: And racism, where's it?

BROWN: That is a struggle.

CALLWOOD: You don't feel it's any better?

BROWN: That is a struggle, and every time you think that maybe we're making progress it flares up again. It's appalling. I heard on the CBC recently that in Germany there's a resurgence of Nazism, and the desecration of Jewish cemeteries is happening all over again as is the whole denial of the Holocaust. People are still alive who lived through that, yet it's coming again.

CALLWOOD: So there's another job. You could start tomorrow. Rosemary, thanks.

BROWN: Don't forget my retirement.

CALLWOOD: Oh, yes, you're retired. I forgot, good for you.

BROWN: Thank you.

Charles Pachter

$\mathcal{N}$othing could be easier than interviewing Charles Pachter. He is a friendly, funny man who brightens a room by merely coming through the door. What his friends know is that he is also a vulnerable, anxious person, riddled with self-doubt. The sadness in his nature makes him anxious to please. Abraham Lincoln, also a wit, once said that he laughed in order to avoid crying, which perhaps explains the dichotomous temperaments of clowns and comedians and such creative people as Charles Pachter.

His versatility is startling. As well as his hugely famous canvases — the Queen in uniform, humourlessly astride a moose, is a Canadian classic — he is a printmaker, essayist, teacher, architectural designer, and muralist. For a brief period he was also a restaurateur and real estate tycoon. This was followed rapidly by a period in which he was flat broke and pursued by rapacious bankers.

Long snubbed by certain critics, who truly wound him with barbs that seem aimed more at his popularity than his art, Charles was elated to announce at the beginning of our interview that the Art Gallery of Ontario was giving him a show in the summer of 1993. That was a sweet victory.

Charles was born in Toronto in 1942 and received a fancy education at the University of Toronto, the Sorbonne in Paris, and the Cranbrook Academy of Art in the United States. As a teenager at summer camp, he met Margaret Atwood, also a counsellor, and they have been friends and collaborators ever since. Their most splendid joint production is a limited edition folio he illustrated of her poems, *The Journals of Susanna Moodie*, which sold for $6,000 apiece.

He has a collection of jokes in his computer, filed according to category, but the puns for which he is famed come wheeling fresh from his free-associating brain. He calls his flirtation with real estate development "ten loft years"; "Monarchs of the North," he called his Queen-on-a-moose series; he dubbed his stylized portrait of the Supreme Court of Canada *The Supremes*. Subway riders in Toronto are familiar with his huge enamel-on-steel mural in the College Street station, which shows the Toronto Maple Leafs and the Montreal Canadiens hockey teams and is titled, *Hockey Knights in Canada*.

He lives most of the year in a former blacksmith's shop on an alley near the Grange in the heart of Toronto. The tall, narrow building is flooded with natural light and has a flower-fringed patio springing from its flank, but Charlie finds it too desolate in winter. In 1993 he found an Art-Deco house in Florida, where he happily enjoys his winters, away from the sooty snow and early dark.

Jacqui Barley, who edits the show to insert the photographs she cajoles from guests, blew the budget on the interview with Charles. She couldn't resist his paintings, which she interspersed in fanciful frames throughout the show; by pushing the technology she even managed details from them. It took her hours to do the edit, finishing sometimes at dawn, but the result was stunning.

One viewer wrote to complain. He said Canada has far better artists than Charles Pachter and he named a few. My response was bland, but what I should have said is that Canada does not hold an artist who cares more about this quarrelsome and wonderful country: Charles Pachter is a one-man Canada Day parade.

CALLWOOD: Now, Charles, I don't want to start off on the wrong foot, but your paintings are not in the National Gallery of Canada or the Art Gallery of Ontario. But your work does hang in subway stations, in the home of Pierre Elliott Trudeau, and in embassies. Millions of people see your work without ever going into a gallery. How can you explain this?

PACHTER: Well, I suppose I should answer the second part of your comment with the good news that I have a show coming up at the Art Gallery of Ontario this summer.

CALLWOOD: Oh good!

PACHTER: Six paintings will be featured in which I've examined the psyche of the founders of Ontario — John Graves Simcoe and his wife — because this is the 200th anniversary of the founding of Toronto.

CALLWOOD: And they're going to hang in the art gallery?

PACHTER: Well, Mrs. Simcoe's drawings are coming from the British Library. She did a portfolio of watercolours of this area, on birchbark, which were presented to George III as a gift when she and her husband left Upper Canada.

CALLWOOD: Elizabeth Posthuma Gwillim Simcoe. Do you know why she was named Posthuma?

PACHTER: Yes. Her mother died in childbirth and her father died six months before she was born. The Simcoes are fascinating people and I want to work more on raising consciousness about them at this particular time.

CALLWOOD: Oh, come on! Let's talk about your big break-through into the establishment.

PACHTER: Well it was really very simple. I just picked up the phone and called one of the curators at the gallery and said "Look, I've been working on these paintings for nearly a decade. You're bringing Mrs. Simcoe's work to the gallery — would it not be a good idea for my paintings to set the stage for this exhibition?" Dennis Reid, the curator, was extremely sympathetic and came over to look at the paintings. I had no idea it could be done so simply. Instead of wringing my hands and wondering whether or not this would be possible, I just decided to take the bull by the horns and call.

CALLWOOD: You would have been there years ago if you'd only made a phone call.

PACHTER: Well, you know, the cult of the outsider is something that works from two sides. The artist can perpetuate the myth. A lot of that depends really on your own feelings of self-esteem and your own ability to deal with the outside world in a certain way. As we know from discussing Robert Hughes's book, *The Culture of Complaint*, complaining is almost endemic to artists; it's endemic to Canadians. With all of the abundance and the good life that we have, we do spend a great deal of our time complaining about a lot of trivial things.

CALLWOOD: And one another.

PACHTER: Yes. Of all the creative fields, the art world is the most mean-spirited. This has been corroborated by many people I know who have been on juries. Perhaps it's because it's such a small field and the pie has to be thinly sliced. Perhaps it's part of our whole dilemma as a nation. There's art, and then there's Canadian art. There's this whole business about internationalism in art — for example, all the fuss that gets made every time the National Gallery buys the work of an American superstar from the pantheon of dead abstract painters. They manage to get to the lowest level of ignorant people who go "tsk, tsk" and say —

CALLWOOD: "My child could do it."

PACHTER: Yes, it's horrible. The real question, I think is, How does a national gallery see itself in terms of the psyche of the nation? Is collecting the great works from other nations part of its mandate, and if it is —

CALLWOOD: That's the right question, rather than whether my child can do this. You started your career in a kind of impudent way by being attracted in almost an erotic way to streetcars. You did a whole series based on the Toronto streetcar. I think that was what launched you as a sensation.

PACHTER: My first work and the work that I would like to go on record as saying is probably more important was from what I call, if I may say this on air, the "fucked-up" period when I was in my early 20s.

CALLWOOD: Is that that angry black stuff?

PACHTER: Yes. There were lots of images of being strangled.

CALLWOOD: Iskowitz did that, too. He had a black period.

PACHTER: I think a lot of artists go through it. In my case it was a semiconscious need to break away, to break out. Without realizing it I depicted being smothered or strangled. I felt overwhelmed and didn't know how I was going to find the freedom that I felt would be necessary for me to exist. The punnish titles of those works, such as *It's Just a Flesh Wound*, *It's Only a Paper Mien*, represent an attempt to cover up. I'm constantly using song titles because I grew up with that in my background. Those works were a bittersweet way of trying to deal with pain. They provided a catharsis, and I was really grateful that I was able to vent my feelings through painting and graphics.

CALLWOOD: But the streetcar was more joyful.

PACHTER: I went off to Calgary for a year and I discovered Canada. In Calgary I was doing mounties and cowgirls and the sky and cow — all of that stuff. It released me from the inner conflict I had experienced in Toronto. I discovered with great joy what an incredible, vast experience Canada can be if you really go for it. I spent a year and a half teaching in Calgary and then I came back to Toronto. It was the late '60s, the period when we were inundated with images about pop art from the States.

CALLWOOD: Warhol was in.

PACHTER: Yes. So were Rauschenberg and Rivers and Wesselmann and Lichtenstein and all the big American stars, who were usually making the covers of *Canadian Art* magazine then, as well.

CALLWOOD: There's nothing like an American on the cover of *Canadian Art (laughs)*.

PACHTER: For whatever reason, as a middle-class kid from Toronto I just turned around and looked at my own background. Some people might analyze the streetcar in terms of its phallic subconscious or whatever, but to me it represented a determination to take an image that was part of my day-to-day life and to aesthetisize it, to put it into magical environments and work with it in that way. I think the image must have been imprinted on my memory in childhood. I can remember sitting at home at the breakfast table and staring at the cornflakes box, which had an ad for a streetcar you could send away for. I remember at the age of five or six clipping out the cardboard coupon and sending away for it, but it never came.

CALLWOOD: So you realized your childhood dream through your art.

PACHTER: Well, there you are.

CALLWOOD: Then you switched to the moose. You did a

whole moose series, which some people found unbearable. Why the moose?

PACHTER: I suppose it was another childhood thing, if you believe in Konrad Lorenz and the theory of imprinting. When I was five years old, I was chosen to play a lost boy at the Canadian National Exhibition. Among the things that I confronted was a pet moose in an animal compound. I can still remember this giant creature and the fur and the sawdust and the smell of it. Now, as part of the iconography, the first time I did a moose was when I put the queen on it. This image resulted from my childhood confusion about the expression "monarch of the North," which I learned in grade school when we studied the moose.

CALLWOOD: I see.

PACHTER: Yes. So I began to examine this ungainly creature. In some ways, by extension, it became an allegory for the Canadian identity. It was big, it was elusive. It looked like it was formed by a committee.

CALLWOOD: And kind of dumb.

PACHTER: Well, I don't know about dumb. I never saw that aspect of it. Whenever there was a shot of it on the TV, it was always galumphing across a lake or swimming with great gusto in the wild, and it seemed to me to be more intrepid than anything else. So I never saw it as a Bullwinkle or as a cartoon figure. It had a poignancy about it as a creature. I once read an amazing story about how wolves down a moose when they know instinctively that it's aged or infirm, and the moose seems to know as well. It's one of these great macabre ballets of nature where they finally surround this thing and down it. They sink their teeth into its flanks. Apparently this has actually been filmed, although I've never seen it. I wasn't aware of this when I created the image, but now I realize that the queen on the moose has a great precedent in art history — the concept of the woman with the beast.

CALLWOOD: You got a lot of flack for that show.

PACHTER: Yes. It was 1973. I was being impertinent and impudent like a lot of artists are in the early stages of their careers. Part of an artist's mission is "getting noticed," which is something so many young Canadians seem to naively overlook. There are a lot of artists out there. At the time I think I did it because it was a delicious *méchanceté*. It was a naughty thing to do, but it got world press headlines. You know, "Monarchists in Royal Rage over Queen on Moose. Threaten to Slash Canvases" — that kind of nonsense. It was a Warhol phenomenon, and it was art. It became a people's thing, and the more noticed it became as a popular icon, the more the arrogant art world ignored it. This may or may not be of interest, but I never sold any of those paintings at the inaugural show in 1973. When the Queen came to Niagara-on-the-Lake to open the Shaw Festival, I happened to live on Shaw Street. So I called my show The Other Shaw Festival. It wasn't until 1980 that I sold the first painting. Seven years went by.

CALLWOOD: That series didn't sell for seven years?

PACHTER: Yes. For seven years. Not one. And today all the major pieces from that show are in private collections and the people who own them do cherish them because they're a part of our folklore. I remember Don Ferguson from the Royal Canadian Air Farce calling me up and saying, "Look, I'm a lapsed Catholic from Montreal. I saw your painting of the queen with wings and a halo, like the Duccio painting from the Quattrocento." He said, "I must have it," and he bought it on time, and he still has it and cherishes it. That's the kind of collector that artists live for. The painting means a lot to him. Bit by bit you get over the torment and the bewilderment if you think you —

CALLWOOD: But you were playing with that moose. There was torment, but you were having a good time with it.

PACHTER: Oh, yes. I mean I did it because I enjoyed doing it. But what I'm refering to is the legendary apathy of the high art world in cases like this. If you make any kind of grand gestures in our culture, if you make any of the players in the art world look redundant because you may have social skills or verbal skills, which artists aren't supposed to have in the cliché definition, then you're in trouble. And that's what happened with me from the beginning. I tried to play "inept neurotic." I tried to go "blah blah blah" whenever I was asked a question because Warhol started all of that. There are many Canadian artists who play it brilliantly.

CALLWOOD: It's a natural talent *(laughs)*.

PACHTER: As you know artists are supposed to be inarticulate and self-effacing. But if you have to repress your own instincts, at what stage in your life do you say, This is who I am, this is what I am, this is what I do and the rest of you are wrong?

CALLWOOD: The titles of your things that are punnish are wonderful.

PACHTER: Well, I have friends who have said to me, Why did you destroy a beautiful image by going and giving us another double whammy with this? referring to the painting of the Supreme Court judges that I did, which is called *The Supremes*.

CALLWOOD: Davenport and Bay is another nice one.

PACHTER: Thank you. Again it's a local pun. But even if you don't get it, you can still look at the painting and enjoy it for its comment on interior coziness versus scary wilderness, which is what it's about — the wind, the waves, and the rain, and then the glass sliding door and the couch set against it as a kind of a barrier. But I'm not supposed to explain my work.

CALLWOOD: Oh, you're not supposed to explain it. Well, you can go blah blah blah. I'll ask you some questions and you can do that.

PACHTER: Let's try that now.

CALLWOOD: All right. The paintings I find surreal and very dear are ones that I don't see a lot of. They're the ones that were inspired by your trip to Japan, especially that dock that goes out in the blue water. Is that all flat blue?

PACHTER: Blah, blah, blah.

CALLWOOD: Is it flat blue?

PACHTER: It's flat blue, but I'll tell you, my quest in painting — and this is why I feel when I got to Japan that I was so confirmed in that — has always been to try to reduce a confused idea to its simplest form. This is much more difficult that it seems, and this is why one has to admire some of the great abstract colour field painters whom the general public don't usually understand. You're working in these realms of pure colour. For people who mistakenly think that art can only be evaluated by the amount of "work" in the painting —

CALLWOOD: They feel they are not getting much for their money if there aren't 17 colours.

PACHTER: That's it. In fact the dock in that image has 12 different greys. But the pure blue, the cerulean blue where the air and the water have melted into one, that's the zen aspect of that piece. To me it's infinity. When I first painted it, I was having some difficulty because I had separated the sky and the water into two different blues. But when I came back from Japan, I found the answer.

CALLWOOD: You joined them.

PACHTER: Yes.

CALLWOOD: I want to switch the subject, because I need to talk about how you became the wonderful person you are. What I want to deal with now is the flowering of C. Pachter. Is it true that you didn't know you were Jewish? Did it slip your mother's mind?

PACHTER: Well, the folklore is rather amusing because I was born in the middle of the war, in 1942, in downtown Toronto in what was then a Jewish neighbourhood. But for whatever reason — we joke about it now — my parents moved up to a predominantly Anglican neighbourhood in North Toronto, where I grew up with wonderful little "majority" kids. My next-door neighbour was John Macfarlane, who is the editor of *Toronto Life* magazine. But I do remember coming home and saying, "How come we don't have pictures of baby Jesus up on the wall like all the other kids?" And my mother would turn to my dad and say, "Harry, say something. You tell him." Although we were Jewish, we weren't exactly observant. I remember I used to think bingo was Catholic because there was a church around the corner where you'd go in and see all those statues of the virgin, and on the floor were all the bingo cards and the little tiddly winks. As a five-year-old I'd run around in the basements of these places and they were all very exotic. So I grew up in a predominately Christian neighbourhood. I remember my grandmother saying, "You must never look a nun straight in the eye or your teeth will get loose." So one day my sister and I were going down the street to the dentist on one of those old Dewitt streetcars with the wood-burning stove when two big nuns got on. We were terrified because they looked at us and we weren't sure whether they'd got us straight in the eye or not. I got to the dentist and sure enough I had a loose tooth *(laughs)*. That's it. I knew it — she'd gotten me right in the eye.

CALLWOOD: You had an experience when you were four years old that could have launched you right into stardom. You mentioned before that you were touring the CNE. You were the star of a little documentary of some kind, I believe.

PACHTER: Yes. It was the era of the *Canada Carries On* documentaries at the National Film Board, those wonderful bombastic black-and-white movies that Lorne Green was narrating about the 20th century and Canada and the postwar boom. I was playing out on the street on Chudleigh Avenue one day when an aunt of mine called my mum and said they were looking for a kid to play a lost boy at the Ex. The next thing I knew

I was being taken down to the CBC in a cab to be interviewed. When we arrived, I was introduced to producer Sidney Newman of all people and director Jack Olsen — this was back in the booming years of the Film Board. Eugene Kash wrote the music for this film. I was just a little four-year-old. I didn't know what was going on. . . .

CALLWOOD: You were cute, though.

PACHTER: Well, I was precocious and fearless. So I guess that's why they picked me. All I remember is being awakened every morning, dressed in the same outfit, and taken in one of those Chrysler woody wagon convertibles down to the Ex, where I had this illusory impression that everything Canadian was glamorous. There was Barbara Ann Scott, and Joe Lewis and comedians Olson and Johnson —

CALLWOOD: And the moose.

PACHTER: And the moose. So I did that for a couple of weeks and became a kind of little Jackie Coogan much to the chagrin of my older sister, who got pushed off into the shadows.

CALLWOOD: But there's a poignant story that goes with this. Didn't you have to cry at some point when you didn't feel like crying?

PACHTER: Yes. Now, how on earth do you remember that?

CALLWOOD: You told me once when we were sitting in a green room somewhere.

PACHTER: As I remember, there was a scene to be filmed where I was in a compound for lost children. There's this shot of me clawing away at this fence, trying to get out, with the nurse looking like a prison warden. In the scene I'm bawling my eyes out. Well, it turned out when the scene had to be shot that day, I was being bubbly and having a good time. And the director said, "Well, what are we gonna do? We've got to shoot this scene." So my mother picked up a hunk of mud and swatted me across the face with it. I began to cry and said, "What did you do that for?" But it was a great shot. So you —

CALLWOOD:　So it took you about 30 years to forgive her.

PACHTER:　Exactly.

CALLWOOD:　But you had a very serious art education. You didn't just flit from one thing to another.

PACHTER:　As a middle-class kid I was lucky. Somehow my parents realized that I had special needs. They really did. I had the music lessons, I had the art lessons, I had the drama lessons. I can remember them saying, "What are we going to do with him?" They knew at an early age that I was already locking myself in my room and painting on the floor when the other kids were out playing hockey. My mother used to get a little angry and, of course, the prevailing joke was, "You want to paint? Paint the bridge chairs. Do something useful."

CALLWOOD:　You'll never make any money painting *(laughs)*.

PACHTER:　Yeah. I remember once just freaking out and saying, "Don't you ever tell me how to make a living." Afterwards I started doing graduation certificates. I learned how to write "olde English" script. I would make 50 cents a certificate, and I ended up making enough money to go to France. I ran off as quickly as I could when I was 19.

CALLWOOD:　How did you know you were an artist?

PACHTER:　I don't think it's something that you know, you just are. You don't choose to be one. For me it was a kind of a hunger. I only felt good when I was creating these worlds from inside my head, when I was externalizing things that I was observing. I've always been an observer. I find great solace in being able to put effort into searching for truth and examining things whose surface has only been skimmed. It's a painful process because sometimes you don't like what you see. But at the same time I'm finding as I get on that I am able to search deeper and deeper for things that I once overlooked. That gives me great sustenance.

CALLWOOD: During the time you grew up most of the art you were exposed to must have been Group of Seven.

PACHTER: Well in high school it was the usual '50s stuff. The teacher would put the daffodil up in front of the class and like a prison warden scream, "Ready, begin! Start work!" We'd all scratch away with our pencils and look up at the daffodil. Then the buzzer would sound and she'd shout "Stop work! Pencils down!" This was —

CALLWOOD: This was art class and freedom of expression *(laughs)*. Well, doesn't that drive the desire to paint right out of you?

PACHTER: Again I was lucky. I had checks and balances. I had the witchy art teacher, but then I would go to my piano lesson after class. My teacher was one of those ladies who was like "Madame Souzatska" — Rachel Cavalho, God bless her. She was the one who took me under her wing. In a way she fed my narcissism unduly. She said, "Darling it's not your fault you're from peasant stock. We'll make a gentleman of you." Like the aunt in *Gigi*, you know. She thought I had great potential, so she said, "You must go to *Frawnce*."

CALLWOOD: She rescued you.

PACHTER: She did. She really did. The value of these kinds of teachers in a child's life should never be underestimated because they can provide a great escape from what may seem to be *étouffant*, as the French say, "suffocating" at home. For me that outlet was magic. I studied with Rachel Cavalho for nearly 10 years. I was the son she never had. She saw things in me that no one else saw. She would take me down to the Royal Ontario Museum and the AGO when I was around nine. I can still feel her hands on my shoulder as she stood me in front of the Rembrandt *Woman with the Lace Collar*. She said, "This is a Rembrandt. It is beautiful. Therefore you must always love it." I was sort of ordered to love it before I knew why. She had a sense of the great painters of the past and —

CALLWOOD: Why did you not go the route of scenery painting? A lot of Canadian artists were great scenery painters at that time.

PACHTER: I did that stuff, too. I went down to the Rouge River Valley with my U of T friend Ed Roman, who's now a famous glassblower living in the Ottawa Valley. We did all that Gauguin, Van Gogh stuff.

CALLWOOD: You went right through Gauguin and Van Gogh, too?

PACHTER: Oh, I sat in Ontario ravines slapping mosquitos on those little stools and getting oil paint all over my pants.

CALLWOOD: Did you do a Picasso with the nose on the side?

PACHTER: Yes. I did that in my third year at U of T. You go through all of those phases and you become more or less an acolyte of whomever they're presenting to you on a platter. There's an early work of mine which is very Braque-like. There's an image, I think, called *Horseforms* in my book which is a prototype for the moose, too. I don't know where that came from, although we did have an art deco picture in our living room of two silver deer with their necks interlocked.

CALLWOOD: I'd like to change the subject for a minute if I may. Some people find it hard to accept that another part of you is a really skilful entrepreneur. Didn't you own about $7 million worth of property for five minutes?

PACHTER: You're close. It was more like $3 million and it was for about a year and a half. Actually, it was longer than that. I call it my "Ten Lost Years." I fell into that in the early '70s. I was struggling with what you could call the male side of me, or the cliché version of the male side of me, versus the female side. I wanted to prove that even though I was an artist, I wasn't an inept neurotic and that I had good business sense. However, I was constantly obliged to stifle it in my chosen field, because the prevailing stereotype, which comes from the 19th century, is that artists are supposed to be shy and awkward and —

CALLWOOD: Very bad with money.

PACHTER: Yes. Now you could never tell that to Michelangelo or anyone from the Renaissance, or any artist from up until the time of the Industrial Revolution. This myth evolved so that even someone like Van Gogh became stereotyped. Bogomila Welsh-Ovcharov, the woman who wrote the essay in my book, has said it just isn't true that Van Gogh wasn't concerned about money. He was interested in whether his paintings sold and how. The point is that it doesn't matter who you are. We're all allotted certain skills. It doesn't matter whether you're a fisherman or a single mother or an artist or a pole-vaulter, either. Some people are good at business and some people aren't.

CALLWOOD: Well, how good were you at business? As I remember it, you were wiped out in about 11 seconds.

PACHTER: No. It didn't really happen that way. I first bought the Artists Alliance Building in 1973, and I kept it for nine years. I was forced to sell it in 1982. But don't forget, I was in my 30s and I hit a really bad recession in 1981.

CALLWOOD: But you owned most of Queen Street West at one point.

PACHTER: There were around 12 properties.

CALLWOOD: On Queen Street West, which is now booming.

PACHTER: Yes, and I was forced to sell them all for far less than I would have gotten had the bank let me hang on another year.

CALLWOOD: Oh, the banks were rotten, weren't they?

PACHTER: Yes, they were. But I say with great pride and humility, I was once the king of Queen. Now I'm the baron of Beverley. I once had a whole bunch of commercial property that was essentially utilized for artists' workshops, and the theatre. I loved being able to transform spaces. It gave me great pleasure to think that we could re-create Montparnasse in Toronto.

CALLWOOD: I loved Gracie's. Tell us about Gracie's.

PACHTER: Well, Gracie's was a restaurant that celebrated things Canadian. It was somewhat tongue-in-cheek, as the best Canadian things usually are. It had Theme dining rooms that were based on Toronto suburbs, like the Forest Hill Room, the Mississauga Room, the Scarborough Room.

CALLWOOD: I never saw such ugly lamps in my life. They were a triumph.

PACHTER: Yes. Well I knew that when my sister from Kingston walked into the Scarborough Room and saw the matching lamps, she'd say, "This I like."

I got it right on. It was SCTV before its day. On the menu we had things like the Caesar salad and the Trudeau salad and whenever a customer would ask what the Trudeau was, the waiter would say it was a little Caesar. We would play around with the menu names. Instead of saying Boeuf Napoleon, we changed it to Boeuf à la mode de Trenton, or Kapuskasing.

CALLWOOD: Didn't you make a terrible drink that you called a Don River that looked like sludge?

PACHTER: That's right. It was beef bouillon and vodka *(laughs)*. Remember that?

CALLWOOD: Sounds wonderful.

PACHTER: We had other drinks called the Gardiner Westbound and Bilingual Grace Bilingue.

CALLWOOD: And you had butter tarts.

PACHTER: Yes, the butter tart is the quintessential Canadian *patisserie* as I discovered, having had a farm up in Oro Township and having gone to the church bake sales. As the croissant is to France and the doughnut is to America, the butter tart is unique to us English Canadians. In fact I was even able to discern different genres of butter tarts. There are Anglican ones, which are crustier. There are Presbyterian ones, which have more raisins, and Catholic ones, which are deeper.

CALLWOOD: Are there Jewish butter tarts?

PACHTER: Yes, they have little bits of poppyseed on them *(laughs)*.

CALLWOOD: Oh, you're making that up.

PACHTER: Yes, I am. That may be something to try.

CALLWOOD: It could be the wave of the future *(laughs)*. Then you began to have these theme events like The Ugly Show.

PACHTER: That was done because I started one of the first artists' co-ops in the city called Artery. I was noticing once again that we were getting the cold shoulder from the press because there's a symbiotic relationship between galleries who pay for advertising in the dailies and —

CALLWOOD: Are you suggesting something here, Charles Pachter?

PACHTER: *Moi?* Yes, in general the commercial dealers are the ones who get the coverage. I was feeling a little badly because many of my serious artists were not getting the coverage they wanted for their first exhibitions. They all thought that "*moi* was the centre of the universe," and wondered why the critics weren't coming to see their work. So for the fun of it we just decided to do this silly thing, which showed what lurks underneath the elegant facade of the art world. I asked artists who would go along with this to submit paintings that were real screw-ups, ones that they'd tried for so long to make work but couldn't. I remember Louis de Niverville giving us a wonderful portrait of a woman with lips that looked like they came from Mars. He said, "Forget it, I can't fix this. Just put it in the show." Atwood gave us an egg cup she made in her ceramic class that had exploded in the kiln.

CALLWOOD: Didn't you also have a little black sambo hot-water bottle?

PACHTER: We had six of them. They were submitted by Colette Whitten. We priced them $1.98 each or all six for $1.98. Not one sold. They were found at a store on Queen Street, and were the worst things anyone could find. We categorized all the submissions in terms of Tasteless, Racist, Scatological, and Sexual. Sure enough, the show hit the papers. We served warm Freshie in garbage pails. The whole thing took place in the hot weather in the unfashionable backyard of the Artists Alliance Building.

Then a year later we mounted the Stunning Show, which was a parody of the Royal Winter Fair *haut* aristocratic art world. The paintings were all $100,000 and more. Of course nothing sold. We got one set of mushroom tartlets from a caterer, and I had some of the gals dress in maids' outfits from the Shaw Festival and go around in a choreographed tableau. Each time someone would go to pick an hors d'oeuvre they would move away just out of arm's reach *(laughs)*. So we managed to serve a thousand people with one plate of hors d'oeuvres.

CALLWOOD: Not all your shows have been tongue-in-cheek. The biggest triumph you've had in recent years was your show in France.

PACHTER: France was my first big retrospective outside Canada. For those who think that I don't usually get government support, I should mention that I was extremely fortunate in getting the support of the Ontario Ministry of Culture and Communications. They were pleased to be able to help me on this because I was offered a spectacular show at the Civic Museum in St. Rémy de Provence, the town where Van Gogh lived after he cut off his ear. It's a gorgeous part of the country, and the French, I say with great deference, treat artists the way Canadians treat hockey players. To them an artist is, *a priori*, a hero. The respect is not always deserved, but it's a wonderful place to be an artist.

CALLWOOD: When I read that your friends and loads of other people flew over and made it a party, I thought that must have been one of the nicest moments in your life.

PACHTER: It was a dream. The feelings of excitement weren't just due to the fact that people knew they were going to go over and get good return on their investment. They were also glad to see the works hung in this museum, to see the true respect that I was getting. I, of course, didn't trust any of this. I was thinking, What's going on? I'm not used to this, I'm so much more used to the sock on the jaw. But God bless them, that's the way the French are. They just have a certain eloquence when it comes to the visual arts. It's part of their culture and part of their history, and they're very impressed by anyone who has made a statement in the field. They called me *Le maître de l'exotisme canadien* — "the master of Canadian exoticism." And, of course, they saw the queen on the moose in a completely different light. They were interested in the whole colonial connection.

CALLWOOD: Did you take some flags?

PACHTER: Yes, they loved them. That was interesting to me because so many who look at the flag image see it only in its literal representation when, in fact, it's about as abstract as any of these big pieces that you see coming into the National Gallery. If you look at it at that level, there are many different ways of seeing it. I was more influenced by the movement of wind and light on the flag than we see usually in its graphic representation. In fact I'm more interested in the image when it is further abstracted out of recognizability. But most of the ones that the public identifies with are the ones in which you can see the leaf.

CALLWOOD: Which one does Pierre Trudeau have?

PACHTER: His flag painting was given to him by the Liberals as a gift when he resigned. It's got a black background, it's very mysterious. It even has a conflicted feel about it, but he was quite taken with it. He's got it hanging in his library, and I have a lovely letter from him. I was quite pleased by that.

CALLWOOD: You've alluded a couple of times to the Charles Pachter who is out in public, but as people who know you well know, you spend an awful lot of your time alone. You paint for days almost obsessively all by yourself, don't you?

PACHTER: Yes. One of the things I'm constantly trying to come to terms with is the necessity for the level of solitude that gives birth to ideas and discoveries. A considerable amount of sheer banal time has to pass before you can push aside the self-pity and the fear that isolation brings and get to that magic time when the inner world takes over and you don't worry about things like meals and night time or whatever.

CALLWOOD: How does an artist working alone day after day know whether or not the work he's producing is good?

PACHTER: You don't, although once in a while something happens, and you realize you've transformed something banal into something enigmatic or mysterious. You do this little jig and you just go *yes*, yes. I had been ploughing through history books and personal letters and diaries and correspondence about the Simcoes. I wanted so much to try and get my head into where Governor Simcoe was at psychologically, this man who had been flustered on so many occasions by Lord Dorchester. Simcoe was a visionary. Coming here following the American Revolution, he had this vision for a new British Arcadia in the heartland of North America. I wanted to see if I could depict him in the way the Americans depicted Washington, as the father — despite his flaws and faults — of our English Canadian society. I worked on several different images, but at one point I started this big 54-inch canvas of him in cameo. It was almost effortless the way it came out, and I just knew after about two hours of working on it to stop. I said, yes, it's right. Some people who have seen it since have been overwhelmed by it. They say —

CALLWOOD: You did it in two hours?

PACHTER: Yes. But I spent two years reading and thinking and doing other paintings around it. Having done one 10 years before, it just came out of me. I knew it was right, it flowed.

CALLWOOD: Another thing I've noticed about your paintings is the different way you depict yourself as you progress through life and as your talent develops. Your first self-portraits are so wistful. There's a tremendous amount of sadness in your early ones. Then there's that awful one you did about yourself when you had lost all your property, the one you called *Recession*. Then there is the triumphant Charles Pachter — *Da-da-dat*.

PACHTER: It had a lot to do with getting my act together and taking it on the road, I suppose. Don't forget I went off to France when I was 19. I spent a wonderfully evocative student year there, which gave me an inner sense of self-confidence that is often being tried here at home. For whatever reason, it's been well-documented that Canadians have this proclivity for eating our own. We live with it, but at the same time we all need to be stroked; we all need to know that somebody cares. Once in a while if you focus in on those who do, it's a healthy thing to do. In my case France is where that happened. But I'm a lot more confident and optimistic about what's going on here in Canada than I used to be. I have learned not to allow a couple of irksome detractors to hit me full face. There's more than that; there are so many wonderful people out there. I spoke in Stratford in June. I was overwhelmed by the people who came, who I never thought would even know who I was outside of Toronto. It was delightful. There was a buzz, there was great dialogue. I just felt vindicated that what I was trying to share with people, they wanted to share back.

CALLWOOD: That's a development because when you're with people you often use the "defensive armour of humour." I think that's Margaret Atwood's expression.

PACHTER: Yeah.

CALLWOOD: You get very funny. I've enjoyed your humour many times, but it also keeps people at a certain distance, doesn't it? It guards your privacy.

PACHTER: I never realized to what degree that is true. Lately I've been asking myself why I like to joke around. I can be funny. I do like making people laugh. It gives me a sense of sharing. But as you say, there are all kinds of undercurrents about making people laugh that are slightly demonic.

CALLWOOD: It's also something that underdogs do. There is a raft of Jewish humour.

PACHTER: Yes.

CALLWOOD: Now, there's a raft of black humorists. I'm not doing psychoanalysis here, but the quipper is sometimes a very sad person.

PACHTER: Well, I would venture to say that in the long run that's not what I'll be remembered for. One of my great heroes is Daumier, the French satirist, who was a brilliant painter. He also suffered much at the hands of the —

CALLWOOD: Philistines.

PACHTER: Well, yes. But I don't have any hidden agenda here. I try to interpret the world I'm part of. I try to come up with new ways of looking at things that we have taken for granted. I take a great deal of personal joy in discovering things about our culture that are treasures to be uncovered, treasures so many people have neglected. My anger comes from the fact that we actually believe that we haven't had an interesting history. How can you have a country like this and not have had an interesting history? Unfortunately we're not great at PR. I've often been condemned for that because I am good at it. If the Americans learned nothing else, they turned George Washington into Jesus Christ. He's been on their money for 200 years. And we haven't done anything for our good old John Graves Simcoe really. I'm wondering whether there's even going to be a stamp for the 200th anniversary of the city he founded. The point is that these people were there for us, and it doesn't matter how multicultural we are, we can all share in this. It happened. It's history. And we have literally repressed it. We haven't learned about it in the way we could have. I came to it by accident and I can't stop being interested in it. I'm beyond the introductory level now. It took me many months before I began to correlate everything. I began to look at what was going on in France during the French Revolution, and what was happening in the States. I saw how all this incredible shuffling took place in North America — the salvage and rescue operation that —

CALLWOOD: You're getting high on Canadian history.

PACHTER: Yeah, and I'm fascinated by it.

CALLWOOD: You're a solitaire and have been all your adult life. How do you take care of yourself?

PACHTER: Well I was uncommonly blessed with an easy self-reliance. I enjoy having good friends at middle to close distance. But I've often struggled with this conundrum about giving so much of yourself over to another human being in order to make a relationship work. I don't want to say that I've failed at it because I don't think it's fair. It was a choice that I made. It's not to say that that chapter's closed. Every decade I live brings something new for me and a new kind of dealing with who I am.

CALLWOOD: But many of us who are in long relationships or short ones use the other person as a way of finding ourselves. We make an adjustment. We say, this is who I am because of the way you are acting to me. But you come in to an empty space, albeit a beautiful one — your house is a charming house — and there's no one to say who you are except you. So you're self-defining all the time.

PACHTER: Yes and no. Because I make consistent efforts to interconnect with a group of eight or 10 close companions, many of whom I've known since childhood. But I would also have to say that your comment is very perceptive, because it's not enough at this stage of my life. I find that confronting my own attempts to define myself not enough. At the same time I have also come to peace with the fact that for many artists, as with many other people, the pursuit of one's work within a framework of solitude is a perfectly natural thing. There are many people who went through life without a significant other and didn't seem to feel that they were deficient because of it. Perhaps we could start with Beethoven, the point being . . . There was a British psychiatrist, named Anthony Storr, I believe, who wrote a book called *Solitude*. In it he talked about how people do achieve their earthly goals through the pursuit of their work, which is a primary thing rather than feeding off the other person's interpretation. Now, I'm not saying one way is better than the other. I'm just saying —

CALLWOOD: No. You're just saying that's the way you're doing it.

PACHTER: Yes.

CALLWOOD: Is there something spiritual that you are developing? Are you living in the minute or —

PACHTER: Well, I certainly have noticed in the last year or two that I'm far less inclined to want to socialize the way I used to. I don't know exactly why that is. I used to tear off to my friends' cottages in northern Ontario at the behest of any invitation. I was the perfect guest. You know, I'd know when to tell the jokes, bring the good wines, help do the dishes, say "Don't bother, I'll look after that." My friends would say, "Oh, he's a terrific guest and he's so entertaining." Then something snapped in me and I just stopped wanting to do that kind of thing. I don't know yet how that void will be filled.

CALLWOOD: Do you have a sense that there's a kind of questing in you? Are you looking for something?

PACHTER: Well, I guess I can tell you that I did go through a minor crisis after the successful years with the shows in France and Germany and then my book coming out. I found it difficult having to deal once again with the reality of the Canadian cultural world, which is limited. There's only so far you can go before you think you're coasting sideways. Then you have to ask yourself, what is the true meaning of ambition, and is getting a work in the National Gallery the ultimate goal? Is spreading yourself out to new places a more important thing? I thought so much about Gauguin going to Tahiti and Van Gogh going south to Arles and Picasso to Antibes, so that yours truly has just bought himself a little studio in Miami, of all places. I suffer from this affliction called SAD, Seasonal Affective Disorder. In the winter when I'm painting, and I lie down at four o'clock or have a cup of tea and I wake up in the dark half an hour later and I know I have to face another 16 hours of darkness, I start to shut down. It's a serious thing. Those who know me well and watch me can see that I'm not my usual self. Watching the leaves disappear and seeing death all around you in nature makes you descend into a kind of fear.

CALLWOOD: Winter is a death.

PACHTER: Yes.

CALLWOOD: I look forward to seeing a series on palm trees. I'm sure they're going to be a delight.

PACHTER: How about *Moose over Miami (laughs)*?

Buffy Sainte-Marie

The story of Buffy Sainte-Marie's life is so unlikely that it is the stuff of legends. Born on a reservation in Saskatchewan, she is a Cree who was adopted by a mixed-blood couple and raised in Maine and Massachusetts. Apparently abused as a small child, she has shut the door firmly on any discussion of what happened to her.

What her mother's good parenting uncovered in her was the intellect of a genius and musical talent to match. Buffy has a Ph.D. in fine arts, as well as other postgraduate degrees in Oriental philosophy and teaching. In the '60s she wrote some of the great protest songs: "The Universal Soldier," a scathing denunciation of war, was a favourite among peace-marchers. Later she won an Academy Award for "Up Where We Belong" from the film *An Officer and a Gentleman.*

Somewhere in between she went back to her reservation and discovered her Cree heritage. Many people thought she had dropped out of sight, but the reservation always knew where she was: she was right there, trying to help native people regain their dignity and self-respect. Children found her on *Sesame Street,* where she appeared for five years to prove that "Indians still exist" and taught them all a few words of Cree.

After 15 years out of the limelight, she emerged with a startling album, *Coincidence and Likely Stories,* which displayed not only such powerful songs as "Bury My Heart at Wounded Knee" and "The Big Ones Get Away" but also revealed Buffy's wizardry with computers. She did the album by herself at her home in Hawaii —

all the voices, all the instruments, one of them a mouth bow — and sent it by telephone, via a modem bounced off a satellite, to her producer in England, where some parts were replaced and bounced back to her.

She calls it an "artist-intensive record." The technology of it baffles me, even though she explained it at the beginning of the interview. However, it was old stuff for her. In 1967 she made a totally electronic quadraphonic vocal album, a first in the record industry. Of late she has become an accomplished computer artist.

She has raised a son, who is now six feet tall. When he was born in 1973, he was given a beautiful name, Dakota Starblanket Wolfchild. She breast-fed him on *Sesame Street*, a first for mainstream television. She has lived for almost 30 years on the tiny island of Kauai, but she's a global citizen who turns up at the United Nations in New York or a village on the edge of the tundra.

Besides writing songs, she is also an essayist of note. In a thoughtful essay about altruism she observed: "There is something working in altruistic people that makes them care. . . . I think when we are involved in acts of compassion, we feel God growing."

CALLWOOD: I'd like to start by talking about your new album, *Coincidences and Likely Stories*. Would you tell me how it was put together electronically, only you'll have to take it down an octave, so that I'll understand.

SAINTE-MARIE: It's not really very complicated. If you had to examine just what's involved in every telephone call, every time you used the phone it would seem very complicated, but what I do in my own little studio at home in Hawaii can be fairly easily explained. When I feel like singing or writing a song, I go into my studio and I attach my microphone to my computer, bypassing tape. I have a Midi set-up, which means that my keyboards are attached to my computer. I play my music into the computer, and when it's the way that I want it, when I have my violin part and my keyboard parts, or my guitar and my voice, sounding the way I want, I dial the number of the record company in London, England. The music then goes via modem down the phone lines, bounces off the satellite, and is recorded on tape in London. To me, that's a much simpler way for an artist to record than to have to go to Los Angeles and wait in somebody else's studio and say, "Oh, can I touch this? Can I touch that?" which is really foolishness. Anybody who's smart enough to drive a car, let alone play a guitar, can operate a Macintosh, which is an artist's computer.

CALLWOOD: Is this music that you can see?

SAINTE-MARIE: Yes, you can see the way it forms. For instance, one of the nicest parts of making this record was to go against the grain of the record business and use real pow-wow singers. I used these crummy old tapes from my own reserve in Saskatchewan that my nephew had recorded at some pow-wow one day. At the beginning of one of the songs called "Starwalker," there's about 10 seconds of ambient sound. You hear bells on people's ankles as they walk around. That came from just an old junky cassette that my nephew made. What I did was I recorded it onto my computer. Then I could "see" the sound and decide how long I wanted it to last. I'd already recorded the rest of the song on the computer, which will also show how loud it is and how soft it is so that I won't deafen anybody with volume. Digital recording is wonderful because it enables me to see the sounds, and then I just put them together the way I want it. That part of it is almost like making a collage. It's a very simple and direct way for an artist to work. When the artist actually has his or her hands on the record, it makes it sound very warm.

CALLWOOD: Who are all those voices on "Starwalker"?

SAINTE-MARIE: Me. Just me.

CALLWOOD: The women ululating in the background — that's you?

SAINTE-MARIE: That's me having a very good time.

CALLWOOD: "Starwalker" is a wonderful song. I hear that it's on reserves everywhere. It has become something of a theme, hasn't it?

SAINTE-MARIE: I don't know. Maybe.

CALLWOOD: Another song, "I'm Going Home," has some odd sounds in it. Isn't there a jet engine in it?

SAINTE-MARIE: Yes. There's a jet in a couple of places. "I'm Going Home" is actually one of the pieces of music I wrote for the film, *Where the Spirit Lives*, which is a Canadian production. It was about Indian kids in boarding schools.

CALLWOOD: It was a controversial film.

SAINTE-MARIE: I don't think it's controversial at all. It's something that just ended. The last boarding school was recently closed, and it's a story that needed to be told because native people, as a group, have all been abused as children. We've all been taken out of our homes and raised in situations where we didn't have parents around. Consequently, many people of my generation, the previous generation, and the one coming up don't know how to parent. Firsthand parenting was something denied to us, as well as our languages, our religions, etcetera. It was truly a terrible time in our history. As a result on most of the reserves in Canada and the United States, you see a group of people who have great holes in their lives. If something weren't missing in their lives, they might be able to go out and earn money; they might be able to go out and get political clout. The something that's missing has to do with self-identity and self-esteem, and it's something that I'm addressing through the arts. I feel as though the arts are the medicine that's needed. We have out-of-work native artists all over the place.

CALLWOOD: You and John Kim Bell have been doing a lot, haven't you?

SAINTE-MARIE: John addresses the problem in a slightly different way. He is primarily involved with helping native people who are interested in going into the arts to get scholarship funding and training. But the people that John's organization doesn't touch, the non-artists, also need the medicine and the healing that the arts bring. So I'm going directly onto the reserves with artists who are unknown. I'm using people who are unknown because my own show involves too much fame and glory. Hopefully by going back week after week to the same reserve with enough native artists, I'll be able to improve the residents' self-esteem and give them a stronger identity. Maybe some of these 13-year-olds will say, "Well, I can't sing with a guitar and write songs, but I can certainly move that amp, and I can dance. And this lighting is beautiful." Because the arts is many things. The arts, in the mainstream, is stars, who are removed from the streets and dangled in front of everybody's noses for money. But that's not what native arts is about.

CALLWOOD: Tell me about native singing. Is the Indian voice a part of the culture?

SAINTE-MARIE: Oh, yes, and it's quite different, of course, from reserve to reserve. We now have a brand new category at the Junos for the music of aboriginal Canada.

CALLWOOD: Wasn't that your idea?

SAINTE-MARIE: I'm the one who got to present the award on television, but creating the category was a collaborative effort. Elaine Bomberry, who is an aboriginal arts activist from Six Nations, and Shingoose, and I went to CARAS together and, as you already know, the answer was yes. The aboriginal category is based not on the fact that we are nice or quaint or deserve it, it's based on record sales. We're selling hundreds of thousands of records across Canada. It's not just Kashtin and me, it's everybody. So there is a native recording scene right now, and singing is a part of it. Sometimes people sing in their own languages. Sometimes they sing in a very traditional way *(sings in a high-pitched tone)*.

CALLWOOD: Where does that pitch come from?

SAINTE-MARIE: It's just something unique to native people, although I've heard the older people say that we were taught to sing by the eagles. That's a nice thought.

CALLWOOD: You said somewhere that when you're putting together a song lyric — and you've put together some great ones — that you're trying to tell a very long story in three minutes. I think you're spectacularly successful with "Universal Soldier."

SAINTE-MARIE: Thank you.

CALLWOOD: You telescoped a lot into the song "Bury My Heart at Wounded Knee," which is on the *Coincidences* album we've been talking about. It's a very powerful, angry song, and the poetry in it is wonderful. That song tells many stories, doesn't it?

SAINTE-MARIE: It does. All of the information that's in that song has been presented before, but I think it's the first time that the information has been strung together, incident after incident, which allows you to see what happened.

CALLWOOD: "Bury me with pretty lies" — there's some lovely poetry in that line.

SAINTE-MARIE: Yes. The [native] people who are so affected by the incidents in that song are gentle people, very gentle, and it is outrageous that such terrible injustices still go on in the world today. It's not that those things only happen to Indian people. I'm involved with the United Nations International Year of Indigenous People. I just got back from the Arctic Circle, from Lapland, where there are Sami people. They are the indigenous people of Scandinavia, who don't get a lot of press. These are people with very white skin, reddish brown hair, and slanty blue eyes, and —

CALLWOOD: No!

SAINTE-MARIE: Yes. I promise — indigenous white people. But they're not truly Caucasian as you would think of southern Scandinavians. They're unique. The Sami are reindeer herders who provided their own teepees for us.

CALLWOOD: The Laplanders are really indigenous people?

SAINTE-MARIE: Oh, yes. Sometimes they're called Laps, but that's not their own name for themselves. They consider themselves Sami people. And there were Inuit people from both Canada and Greenland and —

CALLWOOD: And Russia?

SAINTE-MARIE: Yes, Sami people from Russia. The Sami people are in Finland, Sweden, Norway, and Russia. Although they've been kept apart, especially the ones in Russia, they still speak the same language. What we're talking about in my work, in indigenous peoples' meetings, in the education that I've pursued for myself and tried to share with other people, has to do with the fact that there are still alternatives in the world today. I think it's a helpful thing not to dwell exclusively on race — to realize that there are certain people in the world who don't want Indians or you or me or anybody else interfering with their complete control of all available lands and natural resources. Native people throughout the world are right on the front line of that battle, because their land is where the uranium is, or where the gold was, or where the oil and the silver and the shale are. And so when they're dumping uranium tailings into our side of the river . . . I mean we all belong to that river, you see. But you don't hear about it as soon as I do. So, I packed a lot of that information into that song.

CALLWOOD: "Silver burns a hole in your pocket, gold burns a hole in your soul, and uranium burns a hole in forever. It just gets out of control."

SAINTE-MARIE: It's not a matter of pointing the finger at the bad guy. The point is to understand that there are alternatives to the kind of countries we have now — the United Nations, for instance. I like to think of the guys in the United Nations as all basically being doughnuts. There are all different kinds of doughnuts. Some of them have holes in the middle. Some are filled with very sweet stuff. Some have frosting. There are so many flavours, but they're all basically doughnuts. Sugar and flour and some grease.

CALLWOOD: Some grease *(laughs)*!

SAINTE-MARIE: I don't mean this in a condescending way. Doughnuts are nice.

CALLWOOD: I like them.

SAINTE-MARIE: With the former Soviet countries trying to form new governments, they only look as far as the successful United Nations countries, which are, in my opinion, out of ideas and need fresh ideas. Now, the three most important ideas in the United Nations, which also work in the United States Congress, but not in Canadian or British Parliament, came from the Iroquois Confederacy and other native nations, many of which happened to be matriarchies. Now, the whole idea that one diplomat speaks at a time — that was an astounding idea. Some people still find it difficult, but it does work at the United Nations. The idea that the people can impeach an elected leader was never, ever found in Europe. Also the idea of sovereign nations coming together without giving up their sovereignty —

CALLWOOD: That's Iroquois.

SAINTE-MARIE: They're native ideas. The point is not, "We're so cool, we're Indians." The point is that there are alternatives that have in many ways been stomped out of existence by the European warlord mentality. It's something that Europe is still suffering under. When I'm in Europe, I see people suffering under the class system today.

CALLWOOD: How did such a nice woman as you ever get to be a woman who had trouble crossing the border and had her phones tapped? Why were you viewed in the '60s and '70s by various governments as somebody too dangerous to have around?

SAINTE-MARIE: Well, I think you might be inflating my importance in the situation a little. What happened was after Kennedy died, Johnson came in and he saw how the music scene was. Many of us were part of the student movement and an artist's movement that was truly something special: alternative ideas were flourishing in music, in lyrics, in poetry. You have to realize that alcohol had not really caught on. The drug of the time was coffee. Coffee houses were a wonderful way for people to exchange ideas. It was actually hip to create your own music and to have original ideas. Now what happened right after that, I wasn't aware of. I just thought that —

CALLWOOD: That's about when you disappeared. Was it in 1976 that you went to the edge of the world?

SAINTE-MARIE: No. I quit recording in 1976 when my son was born, but I had disappeared from the American music scene long before then. I was told by broadcasters here, in Canada, that they had received letters from the Lyndon Johnson White House in appreciation of suppressing my music, which deserved to be suppressed. But mine was not the only career that was handled in that way. If you talk to Eartha Kitt, or if you talk to Taj Mahal, there are many artists who were simply put out of business. In show business, somebody can hold you underwater for four minutes, and you're dead for a long time.

CALLWOOD: You popped up on *Sesame Street* at about that time, didn't you?

SAINTE-MARIE: I did. In the '70s.

CALLWOOD: In about 1976 or 1974?

SAINTE-MARIE: Nineteen seventy-four, yes.

CALLWOOD: You did some bridging on that program that was very important for a lot of people. There are adults now who can remember the bridge that you made. Did you really teach Big Bird how to speak Cree?

SAINTE-MARIE: I taught him how to count *(laughs)*. No, I taught the Count how to count in Cree and also in Lakota.

CALLWOOD: In Lakota? Is that the language that was in the *The Man Who Danced with Wolves*?

SAINTE-MARIE: *Dances with Wolves*. Yes, that was Lakota.

CALLWOOD: It's a Cree language, is it?

SAINTE-MARIE: No. No. No. Lakota is totally different. The Lakota are sometimes called Sioux people.

CALLWOOD: You had a baby with you then? What's that child's name? It's got an amazing name.

SAINTE-MARIE: That was my son and his real name is Dakota Starblanket Wolfchild, which Big Bird said was a stuck-up name.

(laughter)

CALLWOOD: It's an amazing name. Does he use it all?

SAINTE-MARIE: No. We've always called him Cody. He's a musician, too. I went on *Sesame Street* again for the same reason. They wanted me to go on to count from one to 10 in English and say the alphabet like Richard Pryor and Burt Lancaster do, but I said no, that I wanted to do it in my language. I thought this was the perfect opportunity to remind little kids, and their caretakers, that Indians still exist, that we're not all dead and stuffed like dinosaurs in museums. We're considered a dead culture by most people, which is such a crime. We're not taken seriously. But that's your loss, because just as Sting is trying to protect the rainforest because there are medicines in there that are probably the cure for something we haven't heard about yet, native people have important further contributions to make. As I said earlier, the three great ideas in the United Nations, the three greatest ideas in government in the world today, came from our people.

CALLWOOD: Well, the message that you got across on *Sesame Street* was that there was something rather splendid about being a native person. Were you aware of that?

SAINTE-MARIE: No. Maybe not splendid, not splendider than you. But certainly I wanted to show that native people have languages, that we have cultures, that we have numbers, that we have family and fun.

CALLWOOD: Where does the name Buffy come from? Is it a made-up name like Cody?

SAINTE-MARIE: *(laughs)* No. That is what they called me when I was little, and Sainte-Marie is the name of the family that adopted me.

CALLWOOD: You were born in Canada, in south Saskatchewan, and then adopted at about what age?

SAINTE-MARIE: As a baby. So I was raised in Maine and I went to the University of Massachusetts.

CALLWOOD: Was it all white?

SAINTE-MARIE: There was one other native in my town, a man who was very helpful to me. He was a Chippewa, and just having him there was a comfort to me, because I had a real rough time as a kid.

CALLWOOD: Were you the only brown face in school?

SAINTE-MARIE: Well, it wasn't that so much as that I was having a really bad time at home. School was just a place to go to vary the humiliation. I came from a family where the men were abusive. They didn't know how to treat a little girl with respect, and they gave me a very difficult time in many ways. I couldn't wait to be grown up and get out of there, even though my adoptive mother was very kind to me. She didn't know about the sexual abuse.

CALLWOOD: She didn't know, or she didn't want to know?

SAINTE-MARIE: I think she did not know.

CALLWOOD: Do you think she would have protected you?

SAINTE-MARIE: Oh, yes. She would have protected me, but she didn't know.

CALLWOOD: How did you maintain your self-esteem with that going on?

SAINTE-MARIE: I had no self-esteem, none whatsoever. I'm an unusual person in that I had music. I've always been an artist. When I saw a piano at the age of three, I sat down and it became my friend. It's been my friend ever since. I didn't have a social life. I didn't play with other kids. I was very frightened. In certain ways, I had a lot of support from my mum, who told me that that's just the way brothers treat their sisters. She didn't know about the other kinds of abuse that were going on in the family. She also told me that when I grew up, I could find out about things that I found interesting in the world. For instance, she used to tell me that Indian people were not as depicted in books, and that when I grew up, I could find out. She was always a help. Oh, she was wonderful.

CALLWOOD: What about sending you to college? Did everybody in your family go?

SAINTE-MARIE: No, I was the first. I was the first in that family ever to go to college. My adopted mum took out a loan so that I could go. She made sure that I at least got to go for one semester. Then it was up to me if I wanted to continue. She said, "You can drop out if you want." She is a wonderful person.

CALLWOOD: That was great. Did you ever tell her what happened?

SAINTE-MARIE: Oh, yes.

CALLWOOD: She must have been horrified.

SAINTE-MARIE: Yes, as a mother myself, I know how hard it would have been for her. She knows what happened. I've been kind in the way I told her about it, and she's been kind in helping me to recover.

CALLWOOD: Was part of recovering going back to your Cree roots? You went back to Saskatchewan in your late teens.

SAINTE-MARIE: Part of my recovery had to do with getting out of the town where those things had gone on, where there wasn't any Indian identity, and where there wasn't any self-esteem for an abused child. I went to college, and when I did, I found out that the world was bigger than that town and that there're all kinds of people in the world, not just the kind that I had been surrounded by. I discovered books and foreign students, and I discovered philosophy.

CALLWOOD: So you escaped into the intellect?

SAINTE-MARIE: No, I did not escape into it. But I discovered that the world was bigger than I had been led to believe, and that it "takes all kinds" in the world. I learned that there were people from many different countries with things to offer me and others. Also I certainly learned that white people are not all monsters, because I have a lot of white education. I went on to get my Ph.D. in fine arts, and I have friends all over the world who have certainly contributed to my somewhat optimistic outlook on this crazy world.

CALLWOOD: It's amazing that you have this outlook. You said earlier there's a hole in the lives of many native people who have suffered that can't be filled. I thought you were also speaking about your own suffering. Many adults who were abused as children can never recover from being very needy and vulnerable people. That element stays with them.

SAINTE-MARIE: Well, being sexually abused can mess you up in many different ways, and that's one of the ways that it shows. It's not the only way.

CALLWOOD: How do you deal with the possibility that you can be victimized?

SAINTE-MARIE: Well, I have been victimized even as an adult, and it's very difficult. The first thing you have to understand about many people who have been abused as children is that they have never learned that "no" means anything, because they'll say no, and the abuse just gets worse. Or they'll say no, and somebody will say, "I'll blackmail you." Or they'll say no and their no won't be taken seriously. Consequently the child doesn't learn the power of no. When my own son was growing up, if he said no he really didn't want to do something, I always sat down and talked to him about it and sometimes he was right. Many times he was right. You'll find that people who have not been taken seriously as children often won't recognize that they're being taken advantage of when a used car salesman harasses them or someone tries to victimize them in another manner.

CALLWOOD: It's a natural situation almost, isn't it?

SAINTE-MARIE: Yes, because victimizers are clever about it. Victimizers in government are clever about it. Victimizers in daily life are clever about it. It's the kind of thing where if you've had a normal life where there is yes and no, the chances are you'll recognize their ruse and say, "Take a hike." But a person who is vulnerable to that kind of victimization probably won't recognize it.

CALLWOOD: It probably makes you more sensitive, though, to exploiters of all kinds. When you spot someone who's trying to take advantage of a situation, it makes you more angry than it would someone who hasn't been through a bad experience.

SAINTE-MARIE: I don't agree with that. I think one of the problems is that sometimes it doesn't make a person angry because that person has been denied the right to have any anger. It's been frightened out of the person, or it's just never come up. It's never worked.

CALLWOOD: It seems to me that you are expressing anger. But you have chosen to do it through the lyrics of your music and through your activism. Those are expressions that have both things in them — love of justice and rage against injustice.

SAINTE-MARIE: Yes. It's interesting. I think it's so unusual for someone described as a native woman to actually have her head together enough to say something that has not been said before in three or four minutes in *this form* that I love. I really find songwriting a challenging form. It was so unusual in the '60s that people labelled me a protest singer. Now, I did happen to write very well-thought-out protest songs so that other people who had never thought about the form before would say, "Oh, yeah, it didn't take very long." It's not like it's a big, thick book. It happens very fast.

CALLWOOD: A fast idea.

SAINTE-MARIE: Yes. But on the other hand, the songs that have made me my money, and the songs that I write most, are love songs. Both "Up Where We Belong" and "Until It's Time for You to Go," which is one of the most recorded songs in the world, are love songs. They've been the ones that, thank God, have allowed me to remain an artist instead of having to work full-time at some other job, which I wouldn't feel as happy doing. I love being an artist. The arts have given me a lot, and you're absolutely right — I do express myself through music. But it's not something that I only express anger through. I express everything through it. I consider music and the arts very valuable medicine for me and for other people, as well. At the moment, I think the human race is going through a transitional stage.

CALLWOOD: You have a theory that we aren't really evolved yet, don't you?

SAINTE-MARIE: Yes. This is true. I think we're very immature. I think most of the problems with the world, with individuals, and with the species can be explained by the fact that we are immature, as are our various races, national origins, and histories. I don't think that many of us can be equated with a third-grader; most of us are still in kindergarten. Now and then we may meet a first-grader. But we're kindergarteners in the sense that we look down our noses at the babies because they wet their pants. We have this unforgiving little kid attitude. However, I think that the good news is that we can grow, we have so much potential. But so long as we're pointing our fingers at each other and blaming others, we're wasting our time. We're not seeing the true alternatives that we have to share with one another.

CALLWOOD: Tell me about how you raised your son so that he might get past kindergarten.

SAINTE-MARIE: I trust him and I trust nature. He's got a good head on his shoulders, and I've learned from him. There's no secret. I listen to him, and if he asks my opinion, I give it to him. If I think he's going totally off track, I'll mention it to him.

For instance, if he's not doing his homework, I'll speak to him about this. But, I don't nag him at all.

CALLWOOD: How can you raise him so that he doesn't become an abusive male?

SAINTE-MARIE: By knocking on his door every now and then if he's treating me badly. It has happened a couple of times, and I just have to let him know that he can't do that to me. For instance, we have a deal that if he's going to be out late he'll call me. If he calls me, then I can go to sleep, because I know he's spending the night with his friend or whatever. But if he doesn't call me, he understands that I'm going to imagine he's been in an accident, and I'll be all nervous. So we make deals together. I think that he has respect for me not only as a woman but also as a musician.

CALLWOOD: He's a musician, too, is he?

SAINTE-MARIE: He's a great musician. Yeah. He's into jazz and hip-hop. He runs several rap bands and plays in a symphony orchestra, as well.

CALLWOOD: Is he in the new album?

SAINTE-MARIE: No. He'll make his own records some day if he wants to. Like me, he loves music. He came by it naturally. He's a better musician than I am in that he can read music and I can't. I'm illiterate.

CALLWOOD: Do you do everything by ear?

SAINTE-MARIE: Sure. That's what it's really about. People could do this before somebody decided to invent music school and notes and things to teach people who are not musicians how to do it, too. But things happen first. The Bible talks about doing the Law without having the Law (Romans). Pardon me for getting back to this. But you know, Columbus came over here when it was the worst possible time for us to have any kind of cultural communication with Europe because it was the time of the Inquisition. Europeans were torturing and murdering each other. It was horrible. So, of course, they did things like that to us. But they didn't understand that the Creator, the Holy Spirit, had been looking after us all this time. They had no idea of that, and many people still don't. When it says in the Bible that we are made in the image of the Creator, I think that means that we're made creative. We create our world, we create our musics, we create our children, we create our lives. That to me is the miracle of all religions and all art.

CALLWOOD: You've created all this music. You have dozens of albums, but you don't read music. It seems like you've come out of an oral tradition and that you're producing brilliant material on an instinctual level.

SAINTE-MARIE: Art is instinctual. It is. If you have little kids in a room like this — here we have pencils and paper, a piano, some pots and pans — the average little kid will keep himself or herself very busy. Yes. A musician like myself will make music on anything, even pots and pans. Artists will create art out of anything, because we know it's fun and because it's how we communicate. We do it on a very instinctual level, like little kids do. Creativity is natural.

CALLWOOD: What's that instrument that you revived?

SAINTE-MARIE: The mouth bow.

CALLWOOD: What's a mouth bow?

SAINTE-MARIE: It's something you make yourself out of a curved stick. You take a curved stick of any size and you put a hole in one end and a hole in the other end. Then you run a string through both ends. I use a metal string so the sound will be nice and loud for concerts. But originally a sinew or fibre or flax would have been used. A mouth bow basically looks like a hunting bow, and sooner or later I think the musician realizes that you can make music on a weapon. To me, this is an incredible paradigm for life.

CALLWOOD: This is a traditional instrument, is it?

SAINTE-MARIE: Well it's found anywhere in the world where there are hunting societies. So, you see, native people all over the world are the ones with a whole lot in common. The anomaly is the European warlord phenomenon, which came down from Rome and which everybody's suffering under. What it is is a group of suits hierarchically run by the guy up here, who tells the guy just below him what to do. That guy tells the guys under him what to do. Everybody else gets told what to do here, and everybody's afraid of the man at the top but still feels competitive, and secretly wants to take over his power. It's a bad system. It's gone about as far as it can go; people are craving freshness. The freshness is available in native cultures.

CALLWOOD: And none of those guys will ever play a mouth bow. We started to talk earlier about you going back to southern Saskatchewan and finding that you really were a Cree and that there were other Crees in the world. How did that happen? Did you know where to go to find your people?

SAINTE-MARIE: Well, they kind of found me, and I was reunited with them when I was in my late teens. I was taken in by my relatives' family. It's a very common tradition among native people that if the family has lost a child, they'll find another child to take that place in the family at some point. There were two such additions in my new Cree family — me and my sister. That's my family now.

CALLWOOD: Did you suffer from culture shock, since you had no knowledge of the Cree way of life or did you feel at home immediately?

SAINTE-MARIE: I felt at home.

CALLWOOD: Did you really? You connected right away with them?

SAINTE-MARIE: Yeah. I think that's probably why they figured that I was the one to take that space in their hearts, because we did connect. It was a wonderful way to resume life and to give and to learn. I learned a lot about native music, for instance, just sitting around with my uncles and aunts around the drum. They didn't speak much English, but, boy, they sure shared music with me. I also learned an awful lot from my dad. He's 95 now, and to this day his job in life, besides playing bingo, has been to go to the prisons and the hospitals and be with people.

CALLWOOD: Is he an elder?

SAINTE-MARIE: Yes. He's never had an ordinary job; he's "always" been an elder.

CALLWOOD: There are chiefs in your Cree family with wonderful names. What are the names of some of your grandfathers?

SAINTE-MARIE: Well, my dad, Emile Piapot, is the son of Chief Piapot —

CALLWOOD: And there's a whole reservation named Piapot.

SAINTE-MARIE: Yes, Piapot Reserve. That was my birthplace. Then on my mum's side of the family, there's Chief Starblanket. My mother was the youngest daughter of Starblanket's youngest wife. But this chief business does not make me an Indian princess. I'm glad you saw *Dances with Wolves*, because that film shows what being an Indian chief is really about. This isn't some guy who has all the power and money. This is often somebody who has given everything away. This is the guy who has so much heart, so much presence of mind and practicality, that he can bring people's ideas into the same room, as sovereign ideas, and let them be seen by one another. This takes a great talent. Chiefs are not like politicians; they were so misinterpreted by European people. And this Indian princess business. Sorry, I never met an Indian prince or an Indian duke. But there are still, and there have been great matriarchs — great women.

CALLWOOD: There are women chiefs all over North America now.

SAINTE-MARIE: Yes, there are.

CALLWOOD: It seems to me that in the recovery process that's taking place among aboriginal people women are pulling the nations together. I see exceedingly strong women, but I see men with the hole in their lives you've referred to. Perhaps I've been chauvinistic and exaggerated the situation.

SAINTE-MARIE: Well, it is hipper now to recognize the women among our people, who are pulling their weight and doing wonderful things. There are some powerhouse women, but there are also some strong men. Men, I think, got an earlier chance to be seduced down the power road. But don't get me wrong, because I appreciate our native politicians. We need them to be able to go head-to-head with whoever comes along.

CALLWOOD: The ones that went to law school.

SAINTE-MARIE: That's right. Our lawyers, our politicians, our doctors. However, by becoming professionals many of them have really just been swallowed up by the system to the point where something is still missing in their personal lives, and in the lives of the people on the reserves. So this gap is what we're addressing now. What's been missing is women in the arts. And that is the heart that's just surfacing now.

CALLWOOD: Just coming out.

SAINTE-MARIE: It really is surfacing, yes. The alternatives that come to women are very different. They see things differently because of all kinds of physical things and because they have a major role in child-rearing. In the original native societies, it wasn't like it is now. Women and children were listened to — not just women, but children, as well. How foolish it is not to listen to children! How foolish it is only to listen to men! The Iroquois Confederacy was a perfect example of a matriarchy.

CALLWOOD: I was told that when they were making a decision in the Iroquois longhouse they started by asking the youngest child. I thought that was just an enchanting idea. To be consulted would confer such dignity and stature upon a child.

SAINTE-MARIE: Well, it's different in the New World. We welcome freshness. We're not afraid of freshness. In the Old World, those old warlords were afraid of anything they didn't control. They were afraid of alternative religions; they were afraid of nature; they were afraid of women; they were afraid of youth because it threatened their power. So these are the things that they tried to destroy.

CALLWOOD: North America's still saturated with those attitudes.

SAINTE-MARIE: Yes, they're still with us today. But I think perhaps that the world is ripening. In my concept of religion, God is always evolving, and everything in the world is always ripening — the trees, the animals, the plants, the oceans. I think many women are ripening and developing a stronger voice. When you know you have something to contribute and you're not allowed to make that contribution, it makes you feel like a fool. How can you not apply this medicine that you have? Generally it seems that native people are stepping forward more, because our voices are ripening. It's becoming obvious that the world is out of ideas. So if we have ideas, we should feel great about bringing them into the global arena. That's why I'm in favour of computers, fax machines, and all of this technology that links people with each other. We've been so shut out on our reserves. Now we can make a contribution, because we've got modems and fax machines and telephones and the arts and still stay home where we're nourished and needed. Communication is a two-way thing, and it's so beautiful when it works right, when the entire human family is involved. It really gets exciting.

CALLWOOD: Given how your life began, you're an astonishingly optimistic woman. You're a yea-sayer, although I maintain that a lot of what you say is nay, too. Who nourishes this in you?

SAINTE-MARIE: The Creator. I'm creative. If you ask a little kid for his opinion, you usually get something that makes a lot more sense than what you read in the newspaper. As a musician, I'm self-taught. I was isolated as a child, and I was encouraged to think that there was more to learn than I was being told in school. I was being told that there weren't any Indians. Then I went to college. I've travelled in the world. I have a lot of life experience.

CALLWOOD: But you were open to do these things.

SAINTE-MARIE: I don't know why anybody isn't.

CALLWOOD: Yes.

SAINTE-MARIE: It's obvious to me that the world is so full of potential. You know, I feel great just petting somebody's kitty. I get pleasure from very simple things. For instance, a bath makes me very excited. I get up, and if it's raining, I say, "Wow, it's raining!"; if it's sunny, I say, "Wow, it's sunny!" Still, I know that there's a lot to be concerned about in the world — for instance, Bosnia. When I was in Europe recently, I was interviewed by a very intelligent woman from Holland. She said, "Isn't it awful that it's human nature for men to rape?" I replied that this has not always been the case. Because I have travelled, because I live not only in one world but in many, I know about alternatives, and they all seem to balance one another out. Now, if you read historical accounts from the 1600s and 1700s about men, women, and children who were captured by Indian tribes, you'll learn that they were all interviewed when they returned to the colonial settlements. Of course, everybody wanted to know, were you raped? The answer was inevitably, no. Do you know how these colonial writers decided to sum that up? They concluded that Indian men had no sexual appetite.

CALLWOOD: That should be an explanation for not being a rat.

SAINTE-MARIE: I think it's very important in these days that people realize that testosterone does not necessarily make a person a killer or a rapist. Unless men realize this, they will feel as though they should be living up to the expectation that men are sexually aggressive, instead of just letting that go and getting on with life. For a native person to commit rape in the 1600s would have been unacceptable. It would have been viewed as something ridiculous, dishonourable, and perverted. So rape is a perversion. It's not part of male human nature. But in Europe, no one had given these intelligent female journalists that news. So just being a carrier of good news keeps me optimistic. I have a nice life in that I meet intelligent people from many different walks of life and also people in need. Every now and then, I have the lovely role of being a bridge between two cultures.

CALLWOOD: You are a bridge, and you do lectures from time to time on the theme that you're on right now, on the possibility of optimism despite the mess we've made of this planet. Is there a yang to the yin? Do you have times when you have to regroup and pull this together again?

SAINTE-MARIE: Oh, yes. But I don't think of that as yin and yang, because I don't really believe in the yang part. I only believe in yin, and unripened yin. I don't believe in a dualistic world of good and evil. I just don't. I think there's unripe and then there's ripe. We're all moving toward that potential. So that's kind of the philosophy that I have. But, yes, I do have to regroup myself. Sometimes when I'm talking to people who are activists, I'll warn them about the danger of burning out. You have to take time for what St. Francis called Brother Mule. You have to feed yourself every now and then, and you have to take care of your body. When I get really discouraged, I go to sleep. If I feel that way, it's usually because I'm tired.

CALLWOOD: I hate to play devil's advocate and throw one of your lines back at you, but don't you have a line that goes, "Love junkies want to change the world that quickly stays the same?"

SAINTE-MARIE: Yes.

CALLWOOD: Well, there is a fatalism in that that you're not expressing now.

SAINTE-MARIE: Well, there is in that particular song, "The Big Ones Get Away," because I wrote it from the point of view of the wife of an extraordinary man who devoted his entire life to being a general. He believed in the flag and he did exactly what he was asked to by Eisenhower, Kennedy, and Nixon. He did exactly what he was supposed to do until one day when he stood up and told the truth about the president of the United States. His life was then ruined. I tried to imagine what it must have been like for his wife, whom I presently got to know. But even before I met her, I put myself in that role. It's really her philosophy that "love junkies want to change the world." "It quickly stays the same," is only a line in the song, because the world does, in fact, grow. It grows very slowly, though, sometimes; other times it seems like it's growing in leaps and bounds. During the 30 years I've been an artist in the public eye, things have changed immensely. They are immensely better in many ways and much worse in other ways. It used to be that five or 10 years ago when I'd use the slogan Protect Mother Earth, as other natives were doing throughout the world, people would think, oh, what a nice little slogan. The Indians are so cute.

CALLWOOD: But the tide has turned.

SAINTE-MARIE: You're right. Now people realize that's not a quaint slogan. Instead they know it's common sense and that it's vitally important. But the change in attitude has only come about because of a variety of people like Sting, and —

CALLWOOD: I don't see you participating in the protest that's going on right now. You're not standing in front of the loggers at this very minute, Buffy Sainte-Marie.

SAINTE-MARIE: Well, only because I can't be because I'm here. I have talked to the people —

CALLWOOD: Have you?

SAINTE-MARIE: Yes. At Clayoquot Sound.

CALLWOOD: But you must be in demand when people need someone to front for a protest. How do you make your decision whether you'll do that or something else?

SAINTE-MARIE: Well, it depends on whether I believe in their cause first, of course. Then it has to do with how busy I am and whether somebody else can cover that base. For instance, in the '60s when everybody was joining Bob Dylan and Joan Baez in the antiwar marches, I was not there, because they didn't need me. I was on the reserves, where they did need me. Nobody was covering that base. So I would sacrifice fame for the true effectiveness of what I can do, where I can actually help. Getting your name in the paper is not what it's about. Sometimes shining the spotlight on local people, who cannot get their names in the paper, is what it's about.

William Hutt

$\mathcal{W}$illiam Hutt, now in his 70s, is the most commanding figure in Canadian theatre, and not just because of his majestic height or the fact that he carries himself like a grenadier on parade. The Speaker of the House of Commons once recognized this wonderful thespian as "one of Canada's greatest actors." The drama critic for the *Times* (London) called him "a giant of the English-speaking stage."

William Hutt is a gracious man who lives in a large, tasteful house in Stratford. He is famed for his courtesy. Though there has always been something aloof about him, a trait that stems from his intense sense of privacy, his kindness and thoughtfulness are immaculate. He goes about his life and his profession with a sense of propriety that gives dignity to everything he touches.

Bill Hutt is remarkable on stage, fascinating to watch even when he is still. He has played all the great parts: 26 seasons at the Stratford Festival in such thundering roles as Hamlet, Lear, Richard II, and Macbeth, and also such choice bits as Justice Shallow in *Henry IV, Part One*, Feste in *Twelfth Night*, and the Fool in *King Lear*. Someone did the arithmetic: Bill Hutt has performed 47 characters in 29 of Shakespeare's plays. Besides that, of course, are the Chekhovs in his life, the George Bernard Shaws, Eugene O'Neills, and Noël Cowards, to mention a few of the great war horses of theatre. He has played almost all the parts in Oscar Wilde's *The Importance of Being Earnest*, including a hilarious turn as Lady Bracknell at the Stratford Festival.

The country has given him every honour it can lay hands upon. He is a Companion in the Order of Canada (the highest rank) and has an Order of Ontario, as well as a number of honorary doctorates and some lifetime achievement awards.

This consummate actor also holds a military decoration for bravery in the Italian campaign during World War II. The most touching moment in the interview on Vision TV came when I asked him about his military experience. Bill always deals with such questions politely but evasively: it is a part of his life that he prefers to keep to himself. When I broached the subject, he was reticent as usual and I prepared to change the subject. Something in his face stopped me. Slowly, haltingly, he began to describe the death of a young soldier who was disembowelled by a bomb.

For a very moving moment, Bill almost could not speak and tears came to his eyes. Then he composed himself and we went on to talk about something else. After he left, thanking everyone in the crew as he is wont to do, we looked at one another in silent acknowledgement that we had been witness to something rare: the dark space within the regally poised William Hutt, and probably many other veterans, where they lock away the horrors.

He has no plans to retire. Why should he? He's at the peak of his game, where he has been for almost half a century.

CALLWOOD: I want to start by talking about your career at Stratford. You've played 40 or so roles in Shakespearean productions, haven't you?

HUTT: Something in that neighbourhood, between 45 and 50. But that doesn't account for the ones that I've done twice or three times.

CALLWOOD: How many plays have you been in?

HUTT: Twenty-nine or 30 out of the canon of 37.

CALLWOOD: Are Shakespeare's other plays unplayable? If you're not in them, I assume they must be impossible.

HUTT: *(laughs)* What a wonderful way of putting it, June. And very flattering, I may say. No, they're not unplayable. I just got too old to do some of them.

CALLWOOD: You're perfect for Lear.

HUTT: Yes.

CALLWOOD: You can do Lear now for the rest of your life.

HUTT: Othello passed me by, and for some reason nobody ever thought that I could do Richard III. I could do Richard II, but not Richard III.

CALLWOOD: Was that because you're too tall?

HUTT: Maybe or maybe it was because I wouldn't look good in a hump.

CALLWOOD: *(laughs)* Yes, and think of how your back would be at the end of the season.

HUTT: Oh, God, yes.

CALLWOOD: Is *Hamlet* the best or *Lear*? You've done them both.

HUTT: I rather agree with A. C. Bradley that *Lear* is Shakespeare's greatest achievement without necessarily being his greatest play. *Hamlet* in retrospect, I think, is a bore, but it is one of those things that every young actor is dying to do, and that usually kills him, anyway. Simply because, according to many people, it is the pinnacle of young parts for young actors in Shakespeare, and after you've done Hamlet, where can you go? It's sort of like being an overnight success in Hollywood. What do you do after that? Just continue on?

CALLWOOD: Who was the best Hamlet, apart from yourself?

HUTT: Oh, I wasn't that good, but the best Hamlet that I have seen?

CALLWOOD: Yes.

HUTT: I don't know that I have seen that many, to tell you the truth.

CALLWOOD: Well, you've seen Olivier.

HUTT: Yes. If you're talking about either film or stage, I would say that Olivier's film performance is the best Hamlet I've seen. Stagewise, I think Chris Plummer.

CALLWOOD: Yes, I saw Chris's Hamlet, too. That was fine. What about the plays that are, relatively speaking, dogs, like *Titus Andronicus* and *Coriolanus*?

HUTT: Well, I did *Titus Andronicus* on two occasions. It was done, I think, in the late '70s at Stratford, and repeated the following year. It was directed by Brian Bedford, who edited it very cleverly so that it worked. Of course, it's a gruesome piece.

CALLWOOD: Oh, awful!

HUTT: I don't think it is Shakespeare's best tragedy, but it does work as a piece of Grand Guignol theatre.

CALLWOOD: You also played Macbeth. Why is *Macbeth* considered such bad luck? In fact, even hearing the name of the play bothers some people.

HUTT: I really don't know. Maybe it is a coincidence that every production seems to be dogged by misfortune, in varying degrees. When I did it with the Canadian Players, on the opening night the set started to fall down, and I was haranguing Shakespeare with my mouth and holding the set up with my hands *(laughs)*.

CALLWOOD: "Into the breach."

HUTT: Yes.

CALLWOOD: It's a great play.

HUTT: It is a wonderful play, though I'm rather inclined to think with some academicians that there is a scene missing somewhere.

CALLWOOD: Do you mean it doesn't hang together properly?

HUTT: Well, somehow the relationship between Lady M. and Macbeth is I think shortchanged, somewhere. It isn't fully explored.

CALLWOOD: You've done two parts in *Lear* and more in some of the other plays. When you're doing different parts in a play you know very well, is there a time when you lose your concentration, because you're so familiar with it?

HUTT: No.

CALLWOOD: Can you be too familiar with something? For instance, when you're playing the role of Hamlet do you watch the actor who's playing Polonius because you know the latter's lines so well?

HUTT: No, that doesn't seem to bother me. In other words, my mind doesn't wander simply because I'm doing the part again. A problem can arise, though, when you're doing a part a second or third time with a different director, who has an entirely different view of the role than you have. Once you've played a role a certain way, it's very difficult to start doing it entirely differently. You can't, because whatever you did initially — it's just like first impressions are the most lasting ones.

CALLWOOD: Yes. You're talking about mannerisms and style and the personality.

HUTT: Thought processes and reactions to certain situations within the framework of the play itself. It isn't just a question of whether you put a teacup down on that line or not. It's a question of how you think about it.

CALLWOOD: And in *The Importance of Being Earnest* first you played two of the male parts and then you did Lady Bracknell. It was a hoot *(laughs)*!

HUTT: Yes. I played both the boys in it, and I also played Canon Chasuble in it, at one point years ago in summer stock, and then Lady Bracknell. The only person I haven't played is Prism. But then I'm too tall for that. I am.

CALLWOOD: Was it fun to do Lady Bracknell?

HUTT: Ultimately, yes. Rehearsing it was not fun, that is to say, it wasn't agony; but it was a very intense rehearsal period because Robin quite rightly said, "These people are not funny."

CALLWOOD: They're taking themselves seriously. Is this Robin Phillips?

HUTT: Yes, Robin Phillips. He wouldn't allow any other members of the company in initially, in rehearsals, and when, towards the end of the rehearsal period, he did allow some of the members in to watch rehearsal, nobody was allowed to laugh. So we went on the opening night wondering if we were ever going to get any laughs at all. And the reason was, as you say, these people take themselves desperately seriously, and if they don't, they're not funny. A lot of productions of *The Importance*, I think, are arch.

CALLWOOD: Who cast you in that? Did you put yourself up for it?

HUTT: No, not specifically, not really. It was in a discussion that Phillips and I were having, because I was the associate director throughout the '70s. We were discussing what to do at the end of his first season, which was 1975. He wanted to do something just for two weeks, and he said, "I want to just examine a play for its value of style." He said, "something like *The Importance of Being Earnest*." I replied — and I meant it facetiously — "Why not? I've always wanted to play Lady Bracknell." Well, his eyes popped.

CALLWOOD: Except for having to shave, you were just fine *(laughs)*!

HUTT: Yes. Then I looked at him and I said, "No, no, Robin. I'm kidding, I'm kidding." He said, "No, I think it's a wonderful idea."

CALLWOOD: It was a wonderful idea, an inspired idea.

HUTT: If there's any justification to it, I do think that Bracknell is asexual to start with, and I'm totally bewildered as to how she managed to have two children.

CALLWOOD: Yes, indeed *(laughs)*.

HUTT: I think one was quite enough for her, and she only managed to have that one by closing her eyes and thinking of England.

CALLWOOD: I first met you when you were in *Tamburlaine*. Tony Guthrie directed it, and we, the Canadians, took it to New York's Winter Garden Theatre.

HUTT: That's right.

CALLWOOD: It was a big deal. I want to tell you about a phenomenon. When I first saw it at the Royal Alex, I said to myself, boy that's an awful play. But after I watched rehearsal after rehearsal, I came to feel it was the most wonderful play on earth. By opening night, I thought it was the production of the century. But, of course, all the New York drama critics were seeing it for the first time, and they said, this is not a wonderful play. However, it was a great romp.

HUTT: It was a romp, and I think it was a wonderful production. It was the kind of production and the kind of play that, for some peculiar reason, British audiences will take to more quickly than American or Canadian audiences. It is not a very good play. It's very unwieldy, to start with, and the story line is peculiar, to say the least.

CALLWOOD: Yes, but look who was in it, though.

HUTT: Star Trek was in it.

CALLWOOD: Yes, William Shatner.

HUTT: Bill Shatner was in it. Colleen Dewhurst, God rest her soul, was in it.

CALLWOOD: She had a double role. She played both a virgin and a harlot. The people who were just spear carriers had two roles. They had two sets of costumes. Well, tell me about Tony Guthrie's directing, because I found him hilarious. Was it fun to be directed by him?

HUTT: Yes, it was fun. He was the first genuine professional to hit theatre in this country. He brought history with him. Up until that time, there was no history in this country of cultural endeavour, certainly not theatrical endeavour.

CALLWOOD: Bob Fulford makes the point very well that the Brits brought us theatre. Tanya [Moiseiwitsch], Guthrie, Michael [Langham], and so on.

HUTT: Well, I would question that rather sweeping generalization. I don't think the Brits brought us theatre, because there was quite a substantial movement working towards establishing a professional theatre in this country right from the time the war ended, when a lot of us were at university.

CALLWOOD: Yes, Straw Hat.

HUTT: The Straw Hat Players, and also Bob Gill who had an important influence on Hart House Theatre.

CALLWOOD: I was misstating what Bob said. He wasn't really saying that the Brits brought us theatre. But he was making the point that I thought you were making, which was that Guthrie's professionalism took us to another level.

HUTT: Indeed, I think that is true. Tony was six-four and he had a personality to match, as everybody knows. He was very witty and could be devastating with his wit at times. I remember in the rehearsals of *Tamburlaine,* he shouted at me one day, "Will you stop walking as if you were knock-kneed, Hutt!" I said, "Tony, I am knock-kneed."

CALLWOOD: Oh *(laughs)*! You're not. You just wanted a good line.

HUTT: No, no, I am slightly knock-kneed.

CALLWOOD: What's Robin Phillips like? Is he quite a different cup of tea? He seems very self-controlled.

HUTT: He's more of a guru than a director. I don't know that he'd like that, but nonetheless he's incredibly perceptive. He seems to know instinctively what you want to do before you actually do it, and in the course of rehearsals will encourage you to do that. Then you suddenly realize, that's what I wanted to do in the first place.

CALLWOOD: He's intuitive, you think?

HUTT: Yes, very intuitive, and I know he does an enormous amount of homework, but not to the extent that it ever becomes etched in stone.

CALLWOOD: He doesn't fight the actor?

HUTT: No, never. Not with me, anyway, not in my presence. I remember him having a very difficult time with dear Susan Wright one day in rehearsal for a production of *New World* by John Murrell. Robin has always believed that Canadians who try to do British accents simply succeed in bringing to stage an accent and no personality. That's why he does not want any Canadians to do British accents. The accent just covers up your personality. But dear Sus was wanting to play this part with an accent, and he was at her for the entire day. She stood up wonderfully well, but he was a bit cruel with her.

CALLWOOD: Who won?

HUTT: They both did. They both won in that Sus simply took the criticism while maintaining her own integrity. She gave up the accent, yes, but she didn't crumble under the battering that went on.

CALLWOOD: He must have known she wouldn't crumble.

HUTT: I think he probably did.

CALLWOOD: That's the nice side of that story. I'd like to change the subject, if I may. I'm wondering what you were like as a little boy.

HUTT: Happy, generally speaking. Adventuresome. I think daring. Egocentric.

CALLWOOD: Well, all children are, so that doesn't help.

HUTT: Yes, that goes with the territory. Probably disobedient, willful.

CALLWOOD: A little unruly?

HUTT: Willful is a better word. I'm a Taurus.

CALLWOOD: Where are you in the family in relation to your siblings? Or are you an only child?

HUTT: No, I had an older brother. He died last September, and I have a younger sister, who's still with us.

CALLWOOD: You're the middle child?

HUTT: Yes.

CALLWOOD: That's a fateful position.

HUTT: Well, so they say, but one can comfort oneself by saying, the youngest is always wrong and the oldest is inevitable.

CALLWOOD: Yes. What did your parents do, and what kind of a childhood did you have?

HUTT: My father started off in the newspaper field.

CALLWOOD: Good choice!

HUTT: Yes, good choice. The first time I was aware of actually who he worked for and what he did was in the late 1920s, early 1930s, when he was managing editor of nine trade publications put out by Consolidated Press.

CALLWOOD: That's a very big job.

HUTT: It was in those days. Then the Depression set in, and around 1934 or 1935, when the crunch came, he wasn't so much fired; the job just simply disappeared.

CALLWOOD: It happens like that in these days, too.

HUTT: Yes, it does. Then for some time he sold insurance, which he hated, but apparently he was rather good at it. Then latterly, he was managing editor of a trade publication associated with the Canadian Lumbermen's Association.

CALLWOOD: Were you comfortably off as a kid?

HUTT: No. I would say we were, at best, middle class. My father was what I would call a good provider, but we weren't rich. In our younger years, when perhaps we would run short, I can remember him saying, "Well, just remember, Bill, there's always corn in Egypt."

CALLWOOD: What does that mean?

HUTT: It means he had something in the bank.

CALLWOOD: Oh *(laughs)*.

HUTT: And my mother was a very shy woman. She was ultra-Victorian. She had a wonderful saying, which I think would make a good title for a musical, "Humour is dearly paid for at the cost of sweetness of mind."

CALLWOOD: Did you have a rather icy upbringing?

HUTT: There were times when you could skate on it.

CALLWOOD: So home was emotionally cool, if I may make an assumption.

HUTT: Yes, I think it was emotionally cool. It wasn't without emotion, but of the two, I think my father was more emotional than my mother. Now, my siblings may have an entirely different view, of course.

CALLWOOD: It's intolerable when they do *(laughs)*. Were you then a loner as a kid, or were you a gregarious boy?

HUTT: I think I was reasonably gregarious. I liked people and I seemed to have friends. I became much more of a loner after I'd gone into theatre.

CALLWOOD: What I'm trying to get at is the kind of sensibility that shapes a person who chooses theatre. Is there a kind of acting out of another world? Were you a kid who lived in your imagination?

HUTT: Yes, I did that. Maybe I was more of a loner than I think I was. It's quite conceivable. But I do remember that the biggest influence on my young imagination was my aunt, my mother's elder sister, with whom I spent quite a number of the first six years of my life. I stayed with her because both my mother and I were sick the minute I was born, with what they called septicemia in those days.

CALLWOOD: Ooh, you usually die of it.

HUTT: Well, apparently I almost did. Then shortly after my mother got better, she became pregnant with my sister. So the initial sickness and the additional pregnancy thrust me into the arms of my aunt, because mother already had my older brother, and I think we were too much for her at times. Consequently I would sometimes spend months at my aunt's place in Hamilton. She was very influential in the imagination department. She would read to me and we would act things out together.

CALLWOOD: She rescued you in a way, didn't she?

HUTT: I think she did in a way, yes.

CALLWOOD: Then how did you wind up in the Army? Was it because everybody was signing up?

HUTT: Yes, I ended up doing it because everybody else did. The only decision I made was that I was not going to be drafted. In other words, if I was going into the army, I wanted it to be my idea, not anybody else's. So I volunteered —

CALLWOOD: Why did you volunteer for the Army? There were more picturesque ways of doing that war.

HUTT: I volunteered basically because my brother had already volunteered. If I was going overseas, I wanted to go overseas with him, in the same unit.

CALLWOOD: You fought in Italy, didn't you?

HUTT: Yes.

CALLWOOD: What did you get a military medal for? They didn't give them to everybody.

HUTT: I would guess because I took a chance.

CALLWOOD: What did you do?

HUTT: *(laughs)* I was asked to volunteer for something, and I did. That was it. You know, there were a few people that I patched up while some bombs were falling around. I'm convinced I got the medal simply because I was willing to take a chance. I volunteered and nobody else did for this particular —

CALLWOOD: Wars are nasty things.

HUTT: Yes.

CALLWOOD: The Italy war and the Scheldt were the two dirtiest wars for infantry in that whole war.

HUTT: They were. Italy was a really dirty war. We were in the battle of Cassino, which was awful.

CALLWOOD: Were you at Cassino?

HUTT: Yes. It was terrible, terrible. I was there up through to the fall of Rome. The interesting thing about the fall of Rome is, once we all got up there, the American army was coming up the west coast, and we all had to stop to let the Americans into Rome first. It was a political decision to let them in first.

CALLWOOD: And the Canadians had been slogging it all winter long. Ahh! Well, I sometimes think that the situation with AIDS now is like what happened in that war. It was my generation and your generation of young people dying. They lose their lives when they're in their prime or even before they've reached their prime. Then you finally become numb to how many people you know have died, or you almost become numb to it. Did you have a sense of the cumulative guilt and grief that is said to characterize the survivors of a war?

HUTT: Well, I was with the Medical Services in the war. It was what you call a light field ambulance. The duty of a light field ambulance is to drive in behind either the infantry or the tanks, whichever is fighting the battle, and pick up the casualties as quickly as possible and take them back to your own headquarters, which would normally be five or six miles back, out of range. So in a way, I suppose I was introduced to death really before I was introduced to life. What you begin to realize when you see body after body after body coming in, in varying states of wreckage, is that you cannot become emotionally involved. Otherwise you cannot do your duty, you just simply cannot. You have to treat everybody, as harsh and cruel as it may sound, as if they're a machine that needs fixing. You have to tell yourself the machine needs fixing as quickly as possible, so that it can go on working, not necessarily go on working in the war, but go on living.

CALLWOOD: Yes.

HUTT: But if you start thinking of it as another human being, it's hard to go on. I can remember when a bomb dropped on our unit. One of the boys who was a cook was lying there. I'll never forget the look on his face. He was lying there and every ounce of his internals were exposed, and he knew what was going to happen. It was an extraordinary moment in time. I think probably that moved me more than anything. It was sort of a seminal moment in the war that I can always go to for the grief. I can't spread the grief, I've got something.

CALLWOOD: That one boy.

HUTT: Yes.

CALLWOOD: When the Vietnam veterans came back, people understood that they were deeply shaken. That didn't happen with World War II veterans though, people thought they'd come back and just go on as if nothing had happened. Most of them did, too. But look, you're still carrying that pain.

HUTT: Yes. It's a long time since I've thought about it. I suppose it's one of those things that just occurs. I don't talk about the war a great deal, I never have. Not because I'm afraid of talking about it, it's just my life has . . . I was thinking about it last night, that having spent five years in the war in my early 20s, I missed the years of experimentation, when you graduate from high school and say, well I think I'll take a couple of years off, see the world, or try this job or that job, and then go to university in a couple of years — just experiment, because there was no hurry to get into anything in those days.

CALLWOOD: No. There were places to go.

HUTT: Yes, places — and things to do, to experiment with. However, because I lost those years, when I got back, I had to concentrate on the thing that I wanted to do. There was no time for experimenting.

CALLWOOD: Why did you go into theatre?

HUTT: I think because of the influence of what I had seen during the war in London on my leaves. That started it. Well, I suppose it really started with the films I saw in the '30s when I would skip high school with Eric House and go to see a lot of films. I was deeply devoted to some of the Hollywood stars in those days. Then when I began to see live theatre during the war, it really intrigued me, because it was real. There was something real about those people up there, and the fact that they could communicate. They could take me places I couldn't go myself. That's what I wanted to do.

CALLWOOD: You wanted to be able to transport other people.

HUTT: Yes, to take them places they couldn't go themselves. To places where my mind has been and my heart has been, and show them something of what has happened.

CALLWOOD: There was no way to learn the craft in this country at that time. You just had to do a sort of apprenticeship, didn't you?

HUTT: It really was that. Well, when I think back on it, Canadian audiences have been enormously patient. They've always sat there while we were learning our craft and said, "Oh, isn't it wonderful — they're all so good!" when really we were terrible, dear!

CALLWOOD: At least you could remember your lines!

HUTT: Yes, I suppose that's true.

CALLWOOD: People used to go backstage and say, "How do you remember all those lines?" or "The costumes were great!" *(laughs)*.

HUTT: Yes.

CALLWOOD: Well, you played the provinces as they say, didn't you?

HUTT: I have been from one end of this country to the other in varying forms. Yes, I have played the provinces.

CALLWOOD: Was it fun, in the early days? Were you part of that gang that came out of Hart House Theatre?

HUTT: Yes, oh, yes.

CALLWOOD: With Kate [Reid]?

HUTT: Yes.

CALLWOOD: And Barbara Hamilton.

HUTT: Yes.

CALLWOOD: And Anna Cameron and —

HUTT: Anna Cameron, the Davis boys.

CALLWOOD: Who were the men? Oh, yes, the Davis boys.

HUTT: All the Davises. Eric House, David Gardner, George McCowan, Ted Followes. We were all there. They were the golden years, apparently.

CALLWOOD: You all caught fire from one another, I think, to some extent. There was a critical mass of young Canadians who wanted to be on the stage.

HUTT: But also Gill had a great deal to do with it. I believe his influence initially has been underrated. He was a wonderful teacher-director — a teacher at a very basic level.

CALLWOOD: When you first walked out on the stage, did you say to yourself, I own it, to use the expression. Did you feel you knew what you were doing from the beginning?

HUTT: No, I didn't. Not initially. As a matter of fact, I've always suspected rather darkly that I didn't have any natural talent, that my talent was manufactured. Learned rather than being intuitive, instinctive. People have contradicted me very generously, but I'm not convinced by them.

CALLWOOD: Maybe you have some of both.

HUTT: I think some of both, probably. But to answer your question about whether I felt at home on the stage at first — because that's a very good question — I would say no. I probably never really felt it was my home until sometime in the '60s.

CALLWOOD: Not until you were well into Stratford.

HUTT: Yes. That, in other words, when I walk on the stage, I am at home.

CALLWOOD: And I know what I'm doing.

HUTT: Well, I don't always know what I'm doing. Even in my own home, sometimes I don't know what I'm doing, but at least I know I'm home.

CALLWOOD: I see. Do you use yourself in every role?

HUTT: I can't help it. I have to.

CALLWOOD: So is there a piece of yourself in everything you do?

HUTT: Well, yes. You know, it is impossible to divorce yourself from yourself. I always view with a certain suspicion these actors who claim that they get on stage and they're totally different people. They're not. They're just the same person in a different set of circumstances. One wants to point out to them, you speak to your husband or your wife or your boyfriend, your minister, your butcher, the kid who delivers your newspaper, quite differently, but you're the same person. You simply have a different attitude to each one of those people, as you have a different attitude towards different situations in life. But you're exactly the same person.

CALLWOOD: One of the things that I remember from that brief sojourn I had with *Tamburlaine* was the great spirit backstage. We hear a lot about actors coveting certain parts and being jealous of one another, but I didn't see that then. I just saw that you were really all friends and cared about one another. Does that mostly happen, or are there unhappy companies, too?

HUTT: Oh, sure, there are unhappy companies. I haven't noticed that jealousy is a rampant disease in the theatre in this country. Backstage there is healthy competition, of course, and the competition nowadays is much more serious than when I started out, because there's that many more young people who want to go into the entertainment industry. Unhappiness within the framework of a company can result largely if the production is not going well, for whatever reason. It may be overdesigned, underdirected. Perhaps it hasn't been cast very judiciously. Perhaps the play is not very good, and everybody's fighting to make something of a silk purse out of a sow's ear. All those things either individually or combined can make a company unhappy. But my experience in this country is eventually there is always the opening night and people have bought tickets to see it, so you've simply got to get on and do it.

CALLWOOD: Kate Reid said that when she was doing *Who's Afraid of Virginia Woolf?* which you've also done, she was crabby. She took on the personality of the main character in that play.

HUTT: I think that's quite conceivable, particularly if you're playing a significant role. I noticed, for instance, that during the course of the evening when I played Lear and was offstage — not that I was offstage that much in *Lear* — I tended to be sort of old and a bit crotchety and stubborn. But it was simply because you brought into your dressing room what you had experienced on stage for a brief moment, and then it would disappear.

CALLWOOD: So you don't take it home with you.

HUTT: No, I don't take it home.

CALLWOOD: In a long run, I would imagine there would be some problem with trying to keep your performance fresh.

HUTT: Oh, dear, yes.

CALLWOOD: I once wrote about Bob Coote, who was in *My Fair Lady* with Rex Harrison. Rex Harrison had the lead, and Bob was Colonel Pickering. They were pals from England, and they would play around with the lines, change them a bit, to keep the performance fresh. Now, that struck me as playing with fire, but does that happen? Have you done that?

HUTT: Oh sure, yes. I have not had a very long run recently. The longest run I had would have been in Edward Albee's *Tiny Alice*, back in the '60s. It was performed at the Billy Rose Theatre and starred John Gielgud and Irene Worth. I was in it for six months. I left it to come back to Stratford that summer. It closed, I think, about a month and a half after I left, not because I left, it was due to close anyway. It was a trying experience to keep that play fresh because it was a very difficult and at times a very obscure play to start with.

CALLWOOD: It was a strange play.

HUTT: A very strange play, and the trial of trying to make it accessible to an audience and to keep it fresh at the same time became almost impossible after a while.

CALLWOOD: Is there an ethic in acting that says that you have to keep trying to make it fresh?

HUTT: Well, James Agate had this saying that the difference between an amateur and a professional is that a professional can act when he doesn't want to, and an amateur cannot act when he does want to *(laughs)*. I don't necessarily agree with the latter part of that statement, but I do agree with the first part, that a professional has to be able to give a performance when he doesn't want to. Now it may not be the best performance ever, but he has to be able to keep it above the trampoline.

CALLWOOD: That's a nice way of putting it. What I was getting at when I asked about the good feeling backstage and the sense of camaraderie in the profession generally is that in some ways it is like a family. When the profession gets together to do a benefit or something like that, there's a spirit of fun. When there's a tragedy, such as Susan Wright's death or the loss of Kate Reid, the grieving is profound. It looks to me like family grief.

HUTT: It is. It is.

CALLWOOD: Do you think about your own mortality?

HUTT: Yes, I do. But there are so many things I still want to do. I don't want to do them all at once, but I do still plan a year in advance, and that keeps me going. I now have more time to enjoy some of the things I glossed over in the younger years. It goes back to what I was saying about coming back from the war, and I suppose my career has consumed my life.

CALLWOOD: You've worked steadily.

HUTT: Not only have I had the fortune to work steadily, but I wanted to work steadily. My career was the most important thing because I had no time to experiment; one had to get at it and do it and keep it going. While doing that, you begin to realize that not only are you taking care of your own career, but your career is paralleling the growth of theatre in your own country. So you begin to feel responsible not only for your own career, but also for the cultural picture of your country, and you begin to develop a sense of history. All that has consumed me a great deal over the years, but in the last few years, since I have — why am I saying, I haven't worked that much? I've been working steadily since last October and have continued until the end of this year.

CALLWOOD: Back to back.

HUTT: Back to back, right. Nonetheless, when I do have some time to myself, I am now looking around. I'm looking at the sky.

CALLWOOD: It's time to smell the flowers, is it, Bill Hutt?

HUTT: That's right, yes. That's it.

CALLWOOD: What are the things you want to savour that you think you missed as a guy fighting in Italy and then as a man who was consumed by his job?

HUTT: The family, for one thing. You've put it wonderfully well, because there is a sense of family in this profession.

CALLWOOD: You're in a big family.

HUTT: Yes, I am part of a big family, and I've had some wonderful siblings in the last 45 years. So I savour those people and the memories of them — those of them that have passed on and the ones that are still there. I mean, to walk on stage and know that you're going to play a scene with Butch Blake is just a joy, because Butch is such a dear, wonderful man; he's endured all this time, and he is history.

CALLWOOD: Yes, and he gives his all every time.

HUTT: Yes, and tries and tries. He's over 85 now, I'm sure. He must be.

CALLWOOD: Is he really?

HUTT: Yes.

CALLWOOD: I mentioned the word *ethic*, a minute ago. How do you steer an ethical course? How do you know this is the right thing for me? I'm not just asking how you choose a role, but also how you make your life choices. What kind of a conscience have you got? Would you call it a strict one or a forgiving one? Are you tough on yourself?

HUTT: I am tough on myself. I am tough on people who have not done their homework.

CALLWOOD: You're a professional.

HUTT: Yes. Within the framework of a very small area of life, I do not suffer fools gladly. If I sense that there's another actor

I'm playing with who really hasn't done enough thinking about what he's doing or a director who clearly hasn't done enough homework, then I get very firm about that.

CALLWOOD: *(laughs)* What do you mean by very firm? Do you say something or do you just turn into an Imperial Highness?

HUTT: An example of the kind of thing I mean occurred when we were touring Russia with *Lear* way back in the early '70s. Part of the contractual arrangement between Goss Concert and our Department of External Affairs was that the company had to stay in a hotel no farther away than about 20 minutes' drive from the theatre in which we were playing. In addition, the hotel had to have a restaurant in it, because our eating habits were different from the Russians' eating habits. When we got to Leningrad, we were taken to a hotel that was clearly on the outskirts of the city and miles away from the theatre, and it didn't have a restaurant. I went down to the manager's office, where the guy from Goss Concert was, and I said to him, "You will move this company out of this hotel by four o'clock this afternoon into another hotel that has a restaurant in it and that is closer to the theatre." The answer that came back through the interpreter was, "Please, Mr. Hutt, don't get excited" *(laughs)*. I replied, "I'm not excited. I'm simply telling you what's going to happen." And at four o'clock that afternoon, 50 members of the Stratford company were moved to another hotel, and 50 Romanians were moved in. All the poor Romanians were saying, "What happened to us? What happened to our reservations?"

That's the kind of thing I will do. For instance, a situation occurred recently where there was a difference of opinion between myself and the director. It was a situation where I really didn't think he had done his homework properly, and he got what I would describe as being on the edge of rude.

CALLWOOD: Which is intolerable.

HUTT: Well, it is intolerable in front of the company.

CALLWOOD: Ah, I see your point.

HUTT: So I just looked at him and said, "I'm going to take a 15-minute break now." Then I walked off the stage for 15 minutes to let him cool down and to let myself cool down, because I didn't want to get into a screaming argument with him in front of the company.

CALLWOOD: You're a person for the proprieties, aren't you? You're famous for your courtesy.

HUTT: Well, I don't think you can really accomplish a great deal by screaming at people. I've worked with directors who scream, and I just simply retire. It squelches any creative juices I have, if somebody's screaming.

CALLWOOD: You're such a contained person. In some ways you're the way you described your mother — not that you're cool, but you're proper, Bill. You're a proper person. Is there a lot going on inside you that doesn't get expressed?

HUTT: Oh, it gets expressed. I just save it for the stage.

CALLWOOD: *(Laughs)* No. You can't save grief and anger for stage, can you?

HUTT: Oh, no, of course not. If I feel grief, I grieve, naturally.

CALLWOOD: What do you do when you're depressed? How do you get out of it?

HUTT: I don't know. I probably sit in my garden.

CALLWOOD: You stay by yourself to get out of it?

HUTT: Yes. But I don't feel that I'm depressed very much, to tell you the truth.

CALLWOOD: You're working all the time.

HUTT: Well, there is that. The most difficult time I had was during the years at the end of the '50s and early '60s when I was in England. The difficulty was lack of work. It wasn't as if there weren't museums to go to see and lots to see in London. The issue was there wasn't that much work.

CALLWOOD: Yes, but you said, you're consumed by being an actor, so —

HUTT: Yes, and I wasn't being consumed.

CALLWOOD: Are you a religious person?

HUTT: Yes. If you're asking me whether I go to church every Sunday, no I don't. But I am a religious person.

CALLWOOD: How would you describe the kind of religious person you are?

HUTT: I have no problem with the existence of God. I remember a wonderful answer that Carl Jung gave in an interview that I saw on television years ago. He was asked, "Do you believe in God?" He thought for a minute, and then he said, "I don't have to believe. I know."

CALLWOOD: Is that your answer, too?

HUTT: Yes.

CALLWOOD: That's a kind of safety, isn't it?

HUTT: Well, if truth is safety, yes.

Maureen Forrester

$\mathcal{W}$hat most people know about Maureen Forrester is her dark, creamy contralto voice, which has thrilled audiences all over the globe. On the concert stage she is a commanding figure, a lovely, splendidly dressed, elegantly shod woman who floods the hall with the beauty and humanity of her songs.

That is the celebrated Maureen Forrester, but there is also the Maureen Forrester who delights in the ridiculous and puts her whole heart into helping causes she cares about. Along with perky, witty Nancy White and the irrepressible Molly Johnson, Maureen Forrester gives the most benefit concerts of anyone in the country.

Now that she is in her 60s, Maureen should probably be conserving her voice and her energy, but she doesn't do either. Sometimes she retreats to a cottage she adores in northern Ontario's lake country, where she allows the peacefulness to soothe her. When she has only a day between engagements, she has been known to make the long drive for the sake of only two hours of soaking in the serenity of the lake. Mostly, though, she is somewhere singing, often for free.

Her Christmas concert at Casey House Hospice has become a tradition. Residents well enough to leave their beds occupy the front row in the lounge in their wheelchairs, with staff and volunteers packed around them to the walls. Derek Bampton accompanies Maureen on the piano as she sings some delicate, little-known songs of great charm before she swings into the Christmas carols.

When that is done Maureen goes upstairs to the rooms where the very sick lie. She stoops beside the beds and says softly, "What would you like me to sing?" The sick one names something and Maureen Forrester then gives a private concert just for that dying person.

She has all the honours the country could heap upon her, beginning with one of the first Companions in the Order of Canada. Though she really couldn't afford to take the time out of her career, then at its peak, she agreed to head the Canada Council in 1983 and served it well for many years. Her first act when she took over the office was to meet every employee.

On April 18, 1994, Maureen Forrester attended the swearing-in ceremony for more than 100 new Canadian citizens that was staged in an auditorium at the University of Toronto. It was Citizenship Day in Canada, and Judge Margarita Okhovati arranged to have the Honourable Sergio Marchi, minister of Citizenship and Immigration, attend, together with such prominent citizens as Knowlton Nash and Alan Borovoy. Maureen was there with them to take the oath of citizenship in a moving reaffirmation ceremony.

The event closed with Maureen Forrester leading the singing of "O Canada." Some wept. It was a moment to seal in memory: new citizens from more than 50 countries lustily joined in a chorus of that most hopeful of national anthems and, leading them on, one of Canada's most beloved and gracious citizens.

CALLWOOD: What I want to talk to you about first is how quickly you can learn music. People envy this a great deal in your profession because most of them practise constantly, but you don't have to.

FORRESTER: Even as a child, I could pick things up very quickly, but I must admit that I would sit at the piano and play one-finger tunes that I'd hear on the radio over and over again. I think you're either born with a good memory or you're not. I know all kinds of people who find it very difficult to memorize. I say to them, "You're not associating things then. Really think of the poetry, don't memorize the sound. Memorize the sense of the poetry and it will stay with you."

CALLWOOD: How can you do that when you're singing in 26 languages?

FORRESTER: Well I know what I'm singing about in most of them. I mean I speak French, having been born in Montreal and having ended up in a very French neighbourhood. Spanish and Italian are easy, and I speak German quite well. When I sing Lithuanian, it's not quite as easy. Everybody always asks me how I learned Lithuanian. I explain that when I had to learn a song in that language Lesia Zubrack, a Canadian singer who is Lithuanian, took me up to this little church and introduced me to this tiny priest. He was about five feet tall and he looked like Santa Claus with a little rim of white hair. He said, "Oh tell me, darling, how many verses you got to learn?" I said, "Eight." Then he bent down and took out a wonderful bottle of homemade wine and two glasses. He said, "For every verse you'll speak good, I give you a glass of wine." I learned Lithuanian very quickly. The wine was great.

CALLWOOD: What about Chinese, though? There's a jump.

FORRESTER: When I was going to China, everybody said, well, you have to learn to sing a Chinese song. I could say a few words in Chinese, but Chinese is very difficult. However, we found somebody here to help me. The sounds in Chinese have pitches to them. So for a singer, I suppose, it's a little easier. I love Chinese and I love the Chinese.

CALLWOOD: You picked up your languages in funny ways. Your French was street French, wasn't it?

FORRESTER: Street French. *Bain ouais.* I had to clean it up when I learned how to sing, especially when I went to France.

CALLWOOD: And you learned German walking around.

FORRESTER: Yes, although I also had some lessons. My first teacher was an English oratorical singer, but my second teacher, Bernard Diamant, was a Dutchman who spoke impeccable German, like most Dutch people do. So I got my German from him and from John Newmark, who played for me for many years. He was from Bremen and spoke very good German.

CALLWOOD: I thought you learned it from John Wayne.

FORRESTER: John Wayne, no.

CALLWOOD: There's a story that you went to John Wayne movies and they were dubbed in German.

FORRESTER: That's actually true, I'd forgotten that story. When I was studying in Berlin, I used to go to the American movies not realizing they'd be dubbed in German. But, of course, I could see what they were saying in English from the way their lips moved, and then I would hear this German come out, which I found very funny. I sort of learned the rhythm of the language from these films, because I knew from the action what was happening. Do you know what I mean?

CALLWOOD: Yes. That's how Otto Preminger learned English.

FORRESTER: Really?

CALLWOOD: Yes. I hope your German's better than his English was.

FORRESTER: My German is very Berlinerische, they tell me. But when I sing in German, it's like when I sing English. I sing much better English than the English I speak.

CALLWOOD: Didn't you learn Italian in a peculiar way, too?

FORRESTER: I started working when I was very young. I believe I was 13. When I started to sing, of course, I had church jobs and all kinds of little jobs to help pay for my lessons. I also worked all day as a telephone operator. The hours of the job made it too difficult to do lessons. So I decided to split my hours. I worked from six o'clock to ten o'clock in the morning and from six to ten in the evening, and took lessons in the afternoon. At work I would mimic all these operators from around the world who I'd speak to. It was lots of fun. I played a terrible trick on my dad and his brother in New Jersey. The switchboard was empty and it was all manual. So I called my uncle in New Jersey and I said *(speaks with French accent)*, "Allo, eez theez Mr. Robert Forrester? One moment, please. Hold the line, Montreal is calling" and then I called my father on another line and said *(speaks with New York accent)*, "Hello, is this Mr. Thomas Forrester? One moment, please. New Joizy's cawlin'," and I connected them. Each of them thought the other had become a millionaire overnight. I was sitting there howling on the switchboard.

CALLWOOD: The story I heard about how you learned Italian was less colourful than that. Something like you learned it from —

FORRESTER: Well, I also worked for an Italian highway paving company in Montreal. I worked the switchboard very early in the morning before office staff got in, and I learned Italian that way. The problem is that if you have a good accent people think you speak the language fluently. But I sort of fake it, although I've gotten better over the years.

CALLWOOD: Why do you have an affinity for singing in German?

FORRESTER: It's the composers — the Schuberts, Schumanns, Brahmses, and Mendelssohns. They worked in an interesting way. First of all, they chose very beautiful poetry and then set it to music. And the words and the cycles, especially Schumann's *Woman's Love and Life*. It's a wonderful cycle and it's emotionally very nice to perform. I'm always turned on by the poetry first. If I don't like the text, I find it very hard to interpret.

CALLWOOD: Well, there's Beethoven's Ninth, which is Schiller's "Ode to Joy." That's so beautiful. But the part for the contralto is not that good, I gather.

FORRESTER: No, because the poor soprano has to scream her lungs out and the contralto is drowned out by the rest of the quartet.

CALLWOOD: You once called yourself a happy peasant. One of the stories about you that startled me is that you'll eat before a performance. Nobody does that. Do you just eat anything?

FORRESTER: Yes, I'm not nervous. I'm never nervous before a performance. I sing because I love to sing and I've studied the music, and what you see is what you get. I haven't got anything else. So if that's your attitude, you give your very best at all times. Granted you may be better at some times than others because you're better rested or whatever. Still, you can't be the best in the world. You can be the best you can be and try to do that all the time, but you can't be the number one of anything. There's always somebody younger waiting in the wings to take your place, somebody who is just that little bit better than you are. So you also have to know when to move over.

CALLWOOD: But Maureen you have to be exceptional to make your debut in Milan at the age of 59.

FORRESTER: Mind you, I played an 80-year-old woman. I'm actually going to Milan again next week. I'm going to do it again in Tanglewood with Seiji Ozawa, whom I adore, and we're doing *Queen of Spades*, exactly what we did when he conducted in Milan. We're doing it semistaged with the Boston Symphony, which is a wonderful orchestra. Then we do it in Carnegie Hall. After that I come home for four days, and then I pack up and go to Orlando to do the same opera with another company. Fortunately, they're both doing it in Russian. Sometimes in Florida they do operas in English. I would hate to do that.

CALLWOOD: To be on the stage at La Scala must be wonderful.

FORRESTER: Yes, it is. It was the most marvellous experience because from the moment you walk in the building you feel everybody is happy you're there. You sometimes hear about opera houses and the meanness, but everybody was pleasant there: the dressers were nice, the doorman was nice, the prompters were great. I've never worked with prompters. That's very difficult because they say the word before you, so you think, Gosh, did I forget to say the word?

CALLWOOD: Are they in a little box?

FORRESTER: Yes and most Italian opera singers use them. Even Mirella Freni, who's one of the most divine sopranos in the world and a superb actress, won't go on stage if there's not a prompter. Every time she's going to open her mouth, the prompter goes, "Five, four, three, two, one." Sometimes you can hear them on broadcasts from the Met. But we don't use prompters in Canada, so you really have to know your work.

CALLWOOD: Have you never forgotten a line?

FORRESTER: Oh, yes, but I can fake in any language. Most good singers can.

CALLWOOD: One time when you were doing yet another benefit, someone had thoughtfully provided a rug for you to stand on. However, you said that singers don't stand on rugs.

FORRESTER: No, it's just like a sponge. It absorbs all the moisture in your voice.

CALLWOOD: Oh, come now!

FORRESTER: Many concert societies wanting to please the artist will put a beautiful carpet beneath your feet. Disaster! The carpet absorbs sound like a sponge, and all singers like to sing on a hard surface.

CALLWOOD: You came to opera late in your career. Many people wonder how that happened.

FORRESTER: Well, when I was young, I couldn't sing the old ladies. The really great acting parts for the low voice are older people, and I wasn't the type, you know. David Warrack wrote me a song called "You Never Let Me Play the Bride." I've sung mothers, maids, witches, bitches, mediums, and nuns, but never the bride. But it is actually true that we play the character roles, and when you're younger, you want to sing Delilah and Carmen and I just didn't have that kind of voice.

CALLWOOD: In *Carmen* you'd play the fortune-teller, wouldn't you?

FORRESTER: I could have played the fortune-teller, but I also could have sung Carmen if I'd pushed my voice up. However, I don't think of myself as Carmen. I could sing Delilah, though, because it's a more biblical character; it's a different type of sexy role, if you will, in my voice range.

CALLWOOD: Do you tire as a mezzo when you stretch your vocal range?

FORRESTER: You do because it's unnatural. I can sing forever if I'm singing in my voice range. You can always sing those high notes, but when you do them, your voice gets worn out because you're using so much support from the diaphragm and the body gets tired of pushing the sound up. So often when I'm listening to a young person sing and they want so desperately to sing a particular aria, I'll say to them, "You know, you have to be secure with any note. You have to be able to sing it even on a bad day. Unless you can sing down on the note, instead of pushing it from below, you really don't have it. You have to have the note above it to know you have the note that you want to sing."

CALLWOOD: Is there a time when you're singing when you know you've done it perfectly?

FORRESTER: There are performances that are magic, usually because you're working with a great maestro like George Szell and the Cleveland Orchestra doing *Semele* or *Das Lied von der Erde* with Bruno Walter and the New York Philharmonic. I've sung with wonderful conductors all over the world. There's always a certain magic in that because the sound of the orchestra is perfect and the conductor knows exactly how to balance the orchestra under your voice. As I said at the beginning, I always try to be the best I can be that day. You can't be more than that and you can't be jealous of other singers because they have something you don't have. You have to be grateful for what you've got.

CALLWOOD: Have you ever had to sing while you were ill?

FORRESTER: Oh, yes. I can sing over a cold.

CALLWOOD: Can you?

FORRESTER: Oh, yes. Anybody can sing over a cold. I think tenors and very high sopranos may have difficulty, though, because they have to have the head really open to float those notes up there, and if your head is all congested, it's very hard to do.

CALLWOOD: You also sang when you were pregnant at a time when pregnant women weren't even working, let alone appearing on a concert stage.

FORRESTER: Well, my manager used to say, "Oh, darling, isn't that wonderful! Oh, we'll just cancel your season and we'll take up next year." I said, "No, pregnancy is not an illness. I've never felt better in my life." And since I made this statement a lot of singers have gone on tour pregnant and fared very well. Not surprisingly, I have musical children. They've given a lot of concerts without knowing it.

CALLWOOD: Some people say that the fetus can hear the music.

FORRESTER: I think they feel the vibration, the rhythm.

CALLWOOD: There's a cellist who knew a piece that he later discovered his mother had played while she was pregnant with him.

FORRESTER: That's quite possible.

CALLWOOD: Isn't it magical to think you're singing to your baby?

FORRESTER: Well, it's part of you, so it must have some memory.

CALLWOOD: Didn't you get to wear such great dresses onstage? Concert singers have wonderful wardrobes.

FORRESTER: I used to spend a fortune having wonderful clothes made. I would spend hours pressing them because they were mostly chiffon and beads. Now I dress much simpler. I wear a very simple dress with nice jewellery. That way you can travel more easily. It's much easier to press a dress that's a shift rather than something made from yards and yards of chiffon.

CALLWOOD: When you sing the same role in three different places, do you have three different costumes?

FORRESTER: Probably, yes. In one opera, Tchaikovsky's *Queen of Spades*, I even get undressed onstage. It's very cleverly done by the girls in the chorus, who are the maids. The character goes from this very tyrannical-looking lady in a two-and-a-half-foot Madame Pompadour wig to a wizened old woman wearing a nightshirt. We did the opera at La Scala with a wonderful director named Andrei Konchalovsky. He was the director of the action film *Runaway Train*.

CALLWOOD: That scene is almost a metaphor in the sense that there's another person inside most of us. We've got the performance person who does everyday things and then there is this other person, either someone scared or someone who is a child. That scene where the majestic, imperious old woman crumbles and becomes a fragile thing, a moral person, seems to me to be a very powerful image.

FORRESTER: Yes, it is actually. Everybody has their weakness. I've seen the strongest people that I know break down. I think people who can cry openly get rid of those pent-up feelings. Many people think it's a weakness to cry, but I think it's good to cry. I cry when I'm happy. Imagine what I do when I'm sad.

CALLWOOD: When I consider the amount of chaos there was in your childhood, partly because of your mother's careless housekeeping, and the lack of privacy in your house, I think that must have been enormously stressful for you, especially since you're such a fastidious person. It seems that as an adult you've put together a completely different kind of life for yourself, one that is calm and ordered. I'm speaking here of your private life, not your professional one.

FORRESTER: You know, life at home was stressful in a way because you could never get away from others. There weren't doors to each room in our house. Instead there were arches. There was a bedroom in the back and a bedroom in the front with only a curtain in between. There was no privacy ever in the house, and I craved to have my own space. I think that's why I moved out early.

CALLWOOD: At the age of 13.

FORRESTER: No, I didn't leave home when I was 13, but I went to work at that age because my father, being a wonderful Scot, never gave me spending money. I took on all kinds of little jobs to make money. I was determined to have my own money. When I started working, I paid my share into the house. But I never regretted doing that because I've learned as much outside school as I did in it. It was a hard time to go to school because the war was on and the young teachers were all either in the armed forces or working in industries relating to the war.

CALLWOOD: They brought back the old teachers, didn't they?

FORRESTER: Yes, and we had a lot of weird boys in the class, who the teacher was afraid of. The teacher would say, "Take out your arithmetic books." The boys would then say, "No, we want to have art." So we'd have art. As a result, I draw quite well.

CALLWOOD: There's a story that as a small child, as a five-year-old, you got on a streetcar by yourself and went on a long ride. Were you trying to escape from the house where you couldn't get any privacy?

FORRESTER: I had delusions of grandeur even then. Before getting on the streetcar, I always had to wait until somebody who looked like she could be my mother got on because they wouldn't let an unaccompanied five-year-old on the streetcar. I'd get on the streetcar and I'd sit reasonably close to this woman, and if she got off, I'd have to get off. If the car was crowded, I'd wait until the end of the line. I don't know if you know Montreal very well, but Cartierville is probably from the other end of Scarborough out to the west end of the city, to Etobicoke somewhere, maybe farther. It was a long car ride, probably an hour. I'd get off at the end, cross the road, and take a car going the other way. But sometimes the car was going to a different neighbourhood. Fortunately, I always remembered my telephone number — it was Amherst 1373 — and my name. So the police would call my mother and my father would have to take the streetcar to pick me up because they didn't have a car. When my dad finally arrived at the other end of the city, I'd be sitting on a policeman's knee, eating an ice cream cone.

CALLWOOD: You weren't afraid?

FORRESTER: No, I loved wandering. I often told Pierre Trudeau that I used to pass his house all the time because the car went through Outremont. There were lovely houses on the hill. I'd say to myself, when I grow up, I'm going to have servants and a cook. I'll say, "Bring me tea. No, I won't have tea. I'll have sherry." I had delusions of grandeur even as a kid.

CALLWOOD: You lived in a world of theatre that you made yourself.

FORRESTER: Yes, and I wanted to live a different life than the hard life my parents lived. My father was a very hard-working cabinetmaker and my mother had little odd jobs, but there were four children, so it was difficult to make ends meet. Then the war came along and my siblings all went off and got married. I was the last one at home.

CALLWOOD: So things were tough. You're famous for how fussy you are about things being clean.

FORRESTER: My mother was the most wonderful woman, but housekeeping was not her favourite chore. She couldn't afford help, so we all did a bit. I have worked hard for what I have, so I take care of my possessions. When one of my children breaks something and says, "Oh, I'm sorry. I didn't mean to do that," that's not good enough for me. I say, "You have to be a little bit more careful. That was something I bought in another country. I'm very fond of it and I'm really unhappy you broke it." So my children have learned to be fairly careful.

CALLWOOD: But you'll put your best things out when you're having loads of tiny grandchildren over for Christmas dinner.

FORRESTER: Oh, yes. I want them to remember that when they went to grandmother's house, she had silver and a beautiful table cloth and candelabra. I want them to remember me that way.

CALLWOOD: You want it to be a magical time.

FORRESTER: Yes, a nice time. I didn't have a grandmother. Both my grandmothers and one grandfather died before I born. I always envied people who went to their grandmother's house to bake cookies or to do things like that.

CALLWOOD: You just revel in being a grandmother, don't you?

FORRESTER: Yes, that's why I have my wonderful place in Muskoka. That's where we really get together because I don't care if something gets knocked over there. We have such a wonderful time. It's very relaxed and the lake is beautiful. We go there all-year round.

CALLWOOD: You're like you are now all the time. You're a performer without being a prima donna at all.

FORRESTER: Oh, that takes too much effort. When you have to live up to your publicity, it's a real bore.

CALLWOOD: I'm sure you have to work with people who can be difficult. Like all professions, your profession must be full of people who are jealous of each other and who behave badly under pressure.

FORRESTER: People who behave badly, though, are insecure. I truly believe they are. Yes, it's a facade. Just in case they do something wrong, they have an excuse: I was upset; you made me worry; you made me do this. It's a bad attitude. If you give your best at all times, that's all anybody wants from you. But you have to come prepared, as well.

CALLWOOD: Because you're world famous, you've worked with many great people. You worked with Pablo Casals and Bruno Walter —

FORRESTER: The greater the person, the more simple and human he or she is. Casals was a wonderful man and so was Bruno Walter. Casals was so sweet. Both those men used to say to me, "How are the children?" We used to take them all down to Puerto Rico. I'll tell you a wonderful Casals story. People always think of him as this wonderful saintly old man, but he didn't always fit this image. Every time he'd come off the stage, there was a great big brown horsehair chair that he'd sink into and everyone would gather around him and tell him how wonderful his performance was. Then somebody would pick him up and carry him to his dressing room. I watched him from afar one day and I thought, he's not that frail. He can conduct a whole performance without falling over from exhaustion. I watched him very carefully and I saw that he was looking at a young woman with a very good-looking pair of legs. I thought that was wonderful. He was 95 years old.

CALLWOOD: You are widely admired and deservedly so. Whose praise means the most to you?

FORRESTER: Well, if a young person, somebody of college age who I can see is nervous, comes up to me after a performance and says, "I . . . I've never had such a wonderful time. I've never been to a serious concert before." I say, "That's the most beautiful thing you can say to anyone. I hope you'll come back." Often they'll say, "Oh, yes, I'm going to go to more concerts." That's the kind of compliment that really means something because you know you've won over another person to classical music.

CALLWOOD: I would have thought you'd have said your peers, someone like Toscanini, who said you've got a great voice.

FORRESTER: Actually you end up not saying much to the conductors you work with a lot. At the end of a performance, you simply say, "Oh, maestro, such a pleasure." He replies, "Oh, yes, my dear." Then you walk off stage together and that's fine. You don't have to say anything. You know they don't want to be praised. They're embarrassed and you don't want them to feel that way.

CALLWOOD: Are there difficult conductors?

FORRESTER: Oh, lots of them.

CALLWOOD: Are they a little crazy sometimes?

FORRESTER: I've never had trouble with a conductor, but problems have arisen in quartets I've been in. It's usually the older opera singers who create a fuss. I remember one man — I won't name him — who was quite set in his ways. The maestro wanted to start partway through a piece, but this opera singer said, "But, Maestro, we have to start at the beginning for the atmosphere." It wasn't the atmosphere, though. His mind only worked from the first note to the end. He had learned by rote and couldn't improvise. But when you get along with conductors, it's really nice. After concerts with Zubin Mehta, in his younger days, we'd all go out and have coffee together.

CALLWOOD: What about Stokowski, who was famous as a womanizer?

FORRESTER: He was wonderful. The first time I met Stokowski I was going to do *Alexander Nevsky*, my first Russian piece. They said the maestro would like you to come to his apartment to rehearse with the piano. I said, oh, wonderful. It was Park Avenue and I went expecting a maid to answer. But this man came to the door. He had a sheath of white hair like a halo and he was wearing a wonderful old-fashioned Russian dressing gown with a fur collar. He said with a heavy Russian accent, "Oh, come een, dahrling. Sit down." He spoke impeccable English, but he always put the accent on. Actually I don't think he was even Russian. He was Polish. Anyway, it was fun. The younger conductors don't pose as much as the older ones. However, the really great, great old ones, the Toscaninis and people like that, didn't have to pose. You were so fearful of them at first. But you never have to be afraid if you come prepared and know your work. If they ask you to change something, you say yes, and you try it. Then they often say, "No, actually, I like it your way better. We'll do it your way." Very often good conductors will do that.

CALLWOOD: There seemed to be real grief about Leonard Bernstein's death.

FORRESTER: Well, everybody loved him. He was the most lovable man and he was friendly to everybody, but I watched him burn himself out over a period of 20 years. He was wired all the time. You felt if you touched a finger, it would crack. He was painfully thin at the end. He just burned himself out with living and conducting and composing.

CALLWOOD: He was distracting to watch as a conductor.

FORRESTER: Yes, he went 115 miles an hour every minute. It was very distracting, but he did produce. You didn't always agree with him, but his output was stunning.

CALLWOOD: What I'm about to say may relate to the metaphor I used of the other person who is inside the person. The person inside you is someone who doesn't want any arguments or confrontations.

FORRESTER: I hate people who argue senselessly, like my mother and father used to do, although I think it was just part of their romance. I used to do it a bit with my ex-husband, Eugene. He's a wonderful man. However, if you had an argument, it went on and on. I'd walk out of the room because I can't bear people who argue all the time.

CALLWOOD: That's some marriage that you don't have with Eugene Cash. The last time I saw the two of you, you were dancing.

FORRESTER: Yes we were *(laughs)*. You know, there are many people who can't live together, but still love each other, and I love him dearly. He's a wonderful, wonderful man. I married him and we had five children, and we have eight grandchildren, and we'll probably end up with 20. He's the world's greatest grandfather. He loves his grandchildren. He brags about them and has all the latest pictures of them. He'll pull them out to show everybody.

CALLWOOD: Oh, he's such a sentimental man.

FORRESTER: It's nice to be able to say, "He's not my husband but he's one of my very dearest friends."

CALLWOOD: That couldn't have been easy in the beginning.

FORRESTER: No. It wasn't easy, but I had to do it for my sanity.

CALLWOOD: And your kids are as solid as rocks.

FORRESTER: Oh, aren't they? They're wonderful.

CALLWOOD: Yes, they are.

FORRESTER: I should mention how I brought them up. I said to my children from the time they were very young, "You be what you want to be, but you have to be able to make a living. You can't expect somebody to support you. I will support you until you finish your education, then you're on your own. If you want to be a garbageman, be a good one." I'll tell you a garbageman story.

CALLWOOD: Okay.

FORRESTER: This is lovely. I moved into a house on Langley, over in Riverdale.

CALLWOOD: Oh, I remember when you moved there.

FORRESTER: Yes. I had very neatly put several green garbage bags full of paper and cardboard out on the front porch when I heard the garbage truck. Because I didn't know what day was garbage day, I grabbed these bags and ran out onto the street. I ran and said to the garbageman up the street, "Excuse me, sir. Can I give you these bags?" He said, "Only if you sing us a song, because I love your voice." I said to myself, that has to be a great garbageman. I love this neighbourhood. He was probably somebody who had another career and wasn't ashamed to be a sanitary inspector to pay the bills. I admired that man.

CALLWOOD: Why does a city woman like you get so much from living in the country? I'm speaking of your home in Muskoka.

FORRESTER: I love the quiet. I very often go up by myself. It's a two-and-a-quarter-hour drive. When I arrive, I'll pour myself a cup of coffee and I'll go out on the deck just to look at the lake. My house is about a third-floor level above the lake, so I can look right down on the lake. It's so quiet. I like to watch the gulls. We also have one lonely blue heron, who must have lost his partner — I guess they mate for life. I like to stay there and just listen to the quiet.

CALLWOOD: That makes it sound like a spiritual place. Are you talking about a spiritual experience?

FORRESTER: Maybe. I think perhaps it's what people do when they go to church and meditate. My communing is more with nature, with the beautiful things of nature.

CALLWOOD: You're going on a big tour soon. Will you give yourself a day in Muskoka to help you get through that?

FORRESTER: I did last week. I drove up in the morning and came back in the evening.

CALLWOOD: You'll make a round trip in a day just to sit there for a few hours?

FORRESTER: Yes. I'll just go up there for two or three hours to sit on the deck and check a few things. I'll empty the mice traps and put down a little more mice stuff.

CALLWOOD: You were taken to church as a child and then you sang in churches. Do you have a sense of God as a result?

FORRESTER: That's hard for me to answer. I believe there's a very strong motivating spirit that moves everyone. I'm not sure if I'd call it God. I don't envision myself going to a heaven where there's somebody who will pat my head and tell me that I did a good job or a bad job. I believe there's something that drives us — an energy — whether it's former people who have been here or something else. I had a very religious upbringing. I believe in my fellow man. Religious people have been very influential for me. But I feel if you live a good life and you're a good person, that's enough. Just giving lots of money to some religious organization is not going to pay your way into where you think you're going. We go from dust to dust. But then again, I'm going to come back as something else, and I have a feeling I've been here before, anyway.

CALLWOOD: You'll come back singing Lieder.

FORRESTER: I'll come back as a bird.

CALLWOOD: You'll be the other blue heron. I want to talk now about all the benefits you do. You're always doing benefits. Very few people in the profession do as many as you do. Why do you do so many?

FORRESTER: Well, sometimes it gets to be a bit much. I've learned to be more choosy. I was the spokesperson for arthritis for five years. I also offer my time to battered women and children. I feel that that's my specialty. I'm a grandmother, so I worry about little children who have special problems. If there's a benefit to support worthwhile causes like those, I'll participate. But I'm not interested in yet another party to raise money for something fluffy or something that doesn't interest me too much.

CALLWOOD: You've done a lot for AIDS.

FORRESTER: Yes. There's nobody in the world who doesn't want to work for AIDS. Many of my friends have died from AIDS, but it's not simply a question of friends losing friends. I care for my fellow man, and it's a disease that has to be stamped out. It's horrible. It's the most horrible thing to watch wonderful young people wither away from AIDS.

CALLWOOD: Tim Jocelyn died from AIDS. You wore an outfit he designed for you.

FORRESTER: Yes, I did. Tim was my best friend's nephew. I wore a wonderful dress he designed to a Canada Day celebration in Ottawa. It's like a straight sheath with a beautiful overcoat like a Japanese kimono on top of it. And all around the edges is a material, all little different colours; it's sort of like stained glass, it's very pretty. It's a wonderful dress to wear to sing in or to walk in. He was a great designer. He also made me something else that really should go in a fabric museum. It's a bolero, a little sleeveless jacket. The material is a patchwork of musical instruments all in beige and salmon.

CALLWOOD: You wore that at his wake.

FORRESTER: Yes, I did. Everybody wore something he'd designed. He also made me a little handbag. He was so gifted.

CALLWOOD: It's stunning. You always do a Christmas concert at Casey House Hospice, and you go upstairs, where the residents are. Do you find that difficult?

FORRESTER: Many people would be afraid to do something like that, but I'm not afraid.

CALLWOOD: No, not afraid. I didn't think that you were afraid of the infection. But it's just that it is so powerful and affecting.

FORRESTER: Most people say, "I couldn't do that. It would break me up." But you have to think of what it's going to do for the person who's dying. It does them good, even though you're sad doing it. People are so afraid to touch anybody who has a disease so I like to put my arms around a person with AIDS and whisper, "Tell me what your favourite Christmas song is." Then I sing it very quietly to them and a lovely sort of beatific look spreads across their face. Perhaps they're remembering their childhood.

CALLWOOD: Music is the biggest trigger for memories, isn't it? A song will just open up a whole part of your life you thought you'd forgotten.

FORRESTER: Yes. Absolutely.

CALLWOOD: You sang "Makushla," didn't you?

FORRESTER: No. That's what my mother used to sing to me.

CALLWOOD: That was your mother's song.

FORRESTER: Yes. She used to sing that often. She would also sing "Turn Ye to Me" and all those sorts of songs.

CALLWOOD: Was she Irish?

FORRESTER: My mother was Irish. She grew up in Belfast. My father was Scottish and I grew up in a French neighbourhood, which is why I can do so many different accents.

CALLWOOD: I see. Well, I've heard that you do $150,000 worth of benefits in a year.

FORRESTER: That's nice to hear.

CALLWOOD: Yes. Somebody once added it up.

FORRESTER: I try not to refuse to do things. As I said, I've become a little choosy, partly because I feel if somebody is giving a benefit, and the same performers are appearing again, people will say to themselves, Oh, I saw them a month ago. Do I really want to go to this? You have to pick new blood so that it's something exciting for people to come and see, even though they're coming to support a good cause. If they are going to pay a lot of money for their ticket, they want to be entertained, as well.

CALLWOOD: Then there's the other benefit you did when you headed the Canada Council?

FORRESTER: Yes, to atone for all my sins. That was the hardest job I ever had in my whole life. But I decided that if I was going to do it, I had to do it right and be fearless. However, you seem to be on the front page damning the government all the time. You have to do this, though, because the squeaky wheel gets the grease. If you yell and scream long enough, they'll pacify you with something. It's important to realize that the arts generate a lot of jobs. It's not just the person on the stage who's employed. There are also the people who make the costumes. Moreover, people have to learn how to relax. We're always telling them they should. Doctors are forever recommending that people go to concerts or the theatre to take their minds off work. We've got to produce the best artists and in order to do so, we must make sure they have the best education. And that's what the Canada Council does. It subsidizes people's education and all facets of the arts, as well.

CALLWOOD: The big issue you took on was that the juries would have to be independent of the government. You had some nasty fights over that.

FORRESTER: Yes, there were some pretty nasty fights. Tim Porteous was reminding me recently that at one early-morning meeting we had, the government representatives said that they couldn't change the jury system and that it would have to stay as it was. I then quietly said, "Well, I guess I'll just have to resign then." Apparently Herb Gray turned absolutely white, because he knew it could be disastrous if I quit when the government had just appointed me. So my response turned them around a little. However, I didn't do it to be facetious. You join the Canada Council thinking, well, I'm going to clean up this act, just like everybody else. This is the most devoted band of people who work for the arts. They often work well into the night, but they don't last more than three years. That's because they get so burned out from having to turn down so many people's applications. They find it heartbreaking and they get so depressed.

CALLWOOD: You gave up five years to head the Canada Council. That's a long time.

FORRESTER: It was a long time. But I've never resented doing it, because it opened my eyes to how lucky I was in my life that the right people came along and helped me at the right time. It made me see how much talent there is out there that gets lost in the shuffle. People who have potential to create great art and who could bring such pride to this country end up doing something else because they get discouraged.

CALLWOOD: Let's change subjects. Arthur Rubinstein said that this is the singer with the Stradivarius in her throat. As a

Stradivarius ages, it just gets more mellow and rich. What happens to a contralto's voice?

FORRESTER: You never lose your voice. You lose the extremes of the range. I used to be able to sing up into a mezzo-soprano range. Those notes don't sound so great anymore, so I eliminate that part of the repertoire. But you never lose your voice. You may lose volume. When you're young, you're more athletic and sound is supported, like an athlete, from the diaphragm, from the body. However, singers never really have to stop singing.

CALLWOOD: Tenors do, don't they?

FORRESTER: They also lose the top range, and if they start pushing, they sing a little flat. As a result, they eliminate that part of their repertoire. Some may then decide to give up while people still remember them as being in fine form. But I sing even when I'm not paid for singing. I walk around singing to myself all day long.

CALLWOOD: The critics say that as you get older your voice isn't affected by your age, but your interpretation is richer.

FORRESTER: It has more depth, perhaps.

CALLWOOD: They also say that you're moving people to tears with the feeling in your voice as much as the words.

FORRESTER: Well, that's a nice thing to say. It's because of the repertoires I sing. The dark voices don't always sing about joy. I sing *Kindertotenlieder, Songs on the Death of Children*, but it's the most beautiful piece because there's a lullaby at the end that goes, "Although my child is gone, I feel those stars in the sky are his eyes, and he's in the hands of God, looking down on me." Isn't that beautiful? Mahler chose very sensitive poetry.

CALLWOOD: If your voice were a musical instrument, it would be a cello. Being musically ignorant, I am not sure if there would be a vast amount of music for a cello, or a vast amount of music for a contralto. Do you have to go and look for this stuff?

FORRESTER: No, and I've had a lot of things written for me. It's wonderful to be the first one to get a crack at a new piece. It's very exciting. When I leave the country, I always try to put a Canadian piece that I like on the program. And if I do a master class — these are clinics attended by people, often teachers, who want to know your secrets — if I'm doing this, I often use a song cycle called *The Confession Stone* [by Canadian composer Robert Fleming], which follows Mary from the birth of Christ to the Crucifixion. She talks to Jesus as if he's an ordinary little boy. She says, "Don't play with Judas and his friends." She doesn't like that boy Judas. She has a funny feeling about him. So it's a very interesting piece.

CALLWOOD: Oh, yes.

FORRESTER: It's a very successful piece. Most singers are very possessive about a work that's written for them. But if you want to further Canadian music, you can't be that way. When I was doing this class at the Cleveland Institute, a lot of teachers were there. So I took a couple of dozen copies of both Canadian works that I was demonstrating, and I offered them to the teachers at the wholesale price. I said, "I know you're going to love the piece —" I had sung it the night before "— when you sing it yourself, and your students will love it, and you'll order more copies." That's the way I further Canadian music.

CALLWOOD: Oh, good for you.

FORRESTER: I call it being a pusher for composers.

CALLWOOD: Here you are, this great Mahler artist, and yet you once got up on the dance stage at the Royal York Hotel to sing pop songs? Was that fun?

FORRESTER: I loved it. I really love funky blues and all kinds of things. When I was growing up, I used to sing those kinds of songs with my friend Ruthie MacLean. In those days you could get a comic-book version of every Bing Crosby or Perry Como song with all the words, but no music. So when the records came out, we knew the text. Since we didn't have any money to go to the movies or whatever, we would sit on the doorstep on hot summer nights and sing all the songs of the day.

CALLWOOD: Aren't there people in your profession who would think that it's beneath your dignity to sing pop songs?

FORRESTER: Not anymore. I think at one time you were pigeonholed. For example, chamber musicians never sang opera. In the old days you had to stick with your specialty. I think if I had to sing the same thing over and over again I would have retired long ago. I mean, variety is the spice of life. I enjoy the challenge of something different. But I need a microphone to sing pop songs.

CALLWOOD: Why?

FORRESTER: Because you don't use the same muscle as you use when you sing operas. If you're singing classical, it's like lifting a sound and supporting it out with your body. It's like weightlifting. If you croon, and just sort of sing to yourself, as you do when you sing pop music with a microphone, it's different. Your basically singing to yourself.

CALLWOOD: What was the happiest time in your life?

FORRESTER: I don't know. I've had so many happy times. I don't worry about getting to be 109 because I'll never make it. I've lost my appendix, my gallbladder. I've got capped teeth. What's next?

CALLWOOD: A piece falls off here and there. Ah, but Maureen Forrester, you'll go on forever.

Farley Mowat

ℱarley Mowat swaggered into the coach house on the sweltering day of his interview and demanded a drink. "What would you like?" Jacqui Barley inquired. As producer, she's the backbone of the show, but she doesn't find catering beneath her dignity, so she provides the crew and guests with such delights as salmon mousse pâté, croissants, and fruit juices. "We have coffee, tea, mineral water . . ." she began.

"Booze!" Farley roared. "I mean, what have you got to *drink*?"

That is Farley Mowat the performer, as he later acknowledged during the interview. Early in his career he discovered that bluster serves handsomely as a cover for his intrinsic shyness. In truth, he now drinks very little but he did accept some peculiar, rare liqueur that Jacqui was able to find in the cupboards of the kitchen. That part of the ritual Farley Mowat entrance completed, we settled down to talk.

All of his numerous books are filled with his passionate respect for life, excluding only human life. He holds the view, not uncommon among naturalists, that humankind is a destructive breed. He is most spectacularly a protector of whales, mountain gorillas, and wolves. In this endeavour, he much resembles Jacques Cousteau, who patrols the seas, and Farley touches the hearts of people who most feel themselves to be an endangered species: Canadians and Russians. I think he has become Canada's most widely read author because he writes with blazing eloquence on one of the great themes of existence: survival. His books are hugely popular in countries where weather tries men's souls, and women's, too.

Farley is married to a tranquil woman, Claire Mowat, who is also a writer. Her books are distinguished by the lucidity of her prose and her gentle, wry view of such events in their lives as living in Burgeo, Newfoundland, for eight years, and travelling abroad with a Governor General, Ed Schreyer, who happens to be a pal.

In summer they live in a remote village on Cape Breton Island, in order, Farley declares, to get away from people. That is bluster, too: he is far too considerate to be a genuine curmudgeon. A year or so ago two elderly women stopped by to ask timorously for an autograph; they wound up staying the night. The Mowats live in winter in the pretty town of Port Hope on Lake Ontario in a small, cosy house where his mother once dwelled.

Farley often came to dinner at our house when our children were small. They remember him vividly as the man who used to wake them up to tell them bedtime stories. Canadians everywhere honour him as a man who tries to wake us all up by telling us stories of the damage we do. I loved doing the interview with my old friend. I think it shows his valiant heart.

CALLWOOD: Farley, in the middle of the night last night, I got out *People of the Deer*, your first book, which was published in 1952. Here's your first sentence. Are you —

MOWAT: Can I stand this?

CALLWOOD: You can stand it. Wait until you hear this sentence from the Introduction. This is the opening sentence of the first book you ever wrote: "On an evening when the sun hovered above the horizon's lip, I sat beside a man who was not of my race and watched a spectacle so overwhelming in its magnitude that I had no words for it."

MOWAT: Good God!

CALLWOOD: Not bad for a young Farley Mowat, eh?

MOWAT: But can you imagine me saying I had no words for it? Since . . .

CALLWOOD: . . . you went on to write so many books *(laughs)*.

MOWAT: Exactly. You can never trust anything I say.

CALLWOOD: Who was that young man who you sat beside?

MOWAT: His name was Ohoto, and he was an Inuit or, as we used to say, Eskimo. He was with me while we saw the migration of the caribou. The great streamers of life that stretched across the whole of the Barren Lands like smoky tendrils of life,

and made the whole thing come to life. I had never seen anything like it, and I never will again. Not very many other human
beings will either because that spectacle is now in the past.

CALLWOOD: What were you doing there?

MOWAT: Well, I'd gone up as a biologist. That is the cover
story. I wanted to go to the Arctic, and the only way I could get
there was to go in the employ of the federal government, if you
could think of a worse way of ever going anywhere *(laughs)*.
But I knew even at that early stage in my career that when
dealing with cement heads you dealt with them as cement
heads. So I ignored everything they told me to do, everything I
was supposed to do. I simply went to the Arctic, to the Barren
Lands northwest of Churchill, Keewatin Territory.

CALLWOOD: What were you looking for? Why were you there?

MOWAT: I was there theoretically to study wolves and caribou.
But soon after I arrived on the scene, I encountered the last
remnants of the Ihalmiut who were a tribe of inland-dwelling
Inuit. They were a caribou people.

CALLWOOD: The people of the deer.

MOWAT: Yes, the people of the deer. They were in a perilous
state. They'd had a terrible winter — several of them — and
most, about half of them, had starved to death. They had been
going downhill for 75 years as a result of their contact with us,
and they were in the last stages. For some reason, which I can't
really explain, I became deeply involved in their plight.

CALLWOOD: You were there for about two years on and off,
weren't you?

MOWAT: Yes.

CALLWOOD: Did you learn to speak the language?

MOWAT: No, they taught me a kind of patois that they invented
for me. They recognized that my limitations as a linguist were

enormous, and they knew I'd never understand Inuktituk. So they selected words for me and cut off the suffixes and prefixes and spoke a kind of pidgin Inuit to me. I thought I was speaking their language. It was marvellous. The illusion was perfect.

CALLWOOD: *(laughs)* Is it true that you once tented near a pack of wolves?

MOWAT: Yes. I'd gone there to study wolves. So in the first season, I tracked down a family of wolves that was living in a hole in a big sandy esker several miles from our cabin. I pitched a little pup tent on another hill overlooking, separated by about half a mile. And there with a huge pair of German binoculars that I'd brought back as loot from World War II I spied on them. I watched them at love and sleep, at eating and at play, and so forth. They put up with all of this with remarkably good grace.

CALLWOOD: Did they know you were there?

MOWAT: Oh, yes, absolutely. In fact I had parked my tent on one of the main trails leading into their den zone. This was a trail that they'd used every night and every morning for hundreds of years to go out to the hunting grounds. So they had to make a little detour around my tent *(laughs)*.

CALLWOOD: Had you inadvertently stationed yourself on their trail?

MOWAT: Yes, it was entirely inadvertent on my part. But they put up with that, too. They just made their little detour around me.

CALLWOOD: So you didn't buy the myth that wolves are terribly dangerous to man even at the beginning.

MOWAT: No. I didn't buy it at the beginning, but I had been indoctrinated by all the mythology that goes on in our society about the wolves being the great destroyers. Everything from *Little Red Riding Hood* on. So the hair at the back of my neck used to stand on end when I found a wolf looking at me. I would think to myself, is he looking at me because he's interested? Or is he hungry? It took a while before I realized that they were accepting my presence. I didn't pose a threat to them; they figured this out very quickly. They accepted my presence as another entity, another living thing. I was no threat to them, so they were quite prepared to accept me.

CALLWOOD: That caribou herd that you saw and that you describe so magically wasn't your first, was it? There's the story of you with your Uncle Frank.

MOWAT: Yes. My first trip to the Arctic was in 1935 when I was 14 years old. I had this old uncle who was a naturalist. He had discovered that the newly built railroad from Le Pas to Churchill would take you right to the edge of the Barren Lands and to the beginning of the great nesting grounds of all the ducks, geese, swans and shore birds who nest in the Arctic. He was an avid egg collector, a real naturalist. In those days, they collected everything they could get, shot everything they could shoot. That's what they did. Anyhow, he took me north sort of as a go-getter boy to go out and catch eggs. I saw my first caribou from the old train, which took three days to get from Le Pas to Churchill and went 15 to 20 miles an hour when it was wide open. It was called the Muskeg Express. You could get out and walk alongside it and beat it to Churchill any day. We were within 30 to 50 miles of Churchill, having come out of the last of the forest and into the first of the Great Plains, the great tundra plains. I was riding in the caboose. They thought it was safer for me there because the rest of the train was a pretty lively spot. It was full of trappers and various people doing various things such as eating, drinking, fornicating, having a hell of a good time. When I heard the old rusty whistle going *whooo-whooo*, I climbed up into the little cupola of the caboose and looked ahead as the train began to slow down. It was stopping because the whole of the railbed ahead of us was submerged under a river of caribou. For an hour the train just sat there while we watched this great flow move from east to west across our front. So that was my first experience with caribou.

CALLWOOD: They call it *la foule. C'est la foule.*

MOWAT: *C'est la foule*, that's what the French Canadians called it. The throng. The great throng.

CALLWOOD: It must be like seeing some kind of magic.

MOWAT: It was, and it's perhaps the last place on earth that one can see large terrestrial animals in this kind of concentration. The great veldt animals of Africa are now reduced to a tattered remnant.

CALLWOOD: They're just a tourist attraction.

MOWAT: Yes, and such animals have disappeared everywhere else in the world. The buffalo, for example, are all gone. But in parts of the Arctic there are still sizeable chunks of this enormous population of caribou. One is in Ungava, believe it or not, which will be destroyed, of course, if they go ahead with the enormous hydroelectric development that they want to do there.

CALLWOOD: You wanted to do something about the destitution you saw, so you started writing. This really has been the engine in you ever since.

MOWAT: Yes. I didn't know then and I didn't really realize for many years why I had this compulsion. I now know. Claire, my wife, has explained this to me. She has been doing explorations into my ancestry, and she discovered that I am descended from a long line of preachers on both sides of my family. There are Methodist preachers on one side, Anglican preachers on the other. So I guess I started subconsciously preaching.

CALLWOOD: Books are your pulpit.

MOWAT: Yes, that's right. And I've been a pulpit-pounder ever since. But what got me, of course, about the Arctic scene that I encountered in 1947 was the enormous injustice of what we people who had power, the white race, the technological race, were doing to those who had no power. I had not understood this before. Even though I'd just come through a war, I still didn't understand it. But I understood it when I saw the juxta-position of the caribou and the caribou people, who were inti-mately interlocked. I realized that they were one and that under the influence of our desecrations, both were being destroyed. So I got angry, and wrote *People of the Deer*. Then I followed that with a sequel called *The Desperate People*.

CALLWOOD: Now you were the first to blow the whistle and say that we were doing something appalling to native people. Others had made noises about this, but you were the first to make any impact. Weren't you called a liar by someone in the House of Commons? I believe there was a huge uproar there.

MOWAT: Yes. I didn't fool around when I decided to take on the establishment. I took it all on. I took on the Roman Catholic church, the Anglican church, the Oblate missions, the Hudson's Bay Company, the Royal Canadian Mounted Police, and the government of Canada. I said that they were all a bunch of bas-tards, that they were destroying these people and the North. I said they had no right to be there and that we should throw them out and let the northerns have their own country back. Now I was really well ahead of my time.

So this message was not received with great delight in high places. The then minister of Northern Affairs and Resources, as I believe it was called then, made a great speech in the House of Commons and said that I was a total and absolute unmitigated liar. The Eskimos that I wrote about didn't exist. They never had existed.

CALLWOOD: *(laughs)* Pretty soon they won't. That's —

MOWAT: Well, that was true enough. They weren't going to exist for very long. All they had to do was maintain that lie a little longer and he'd be right. Stories were told that I had writ-ten most of the book in a beer parlour at Le Pas. They gave me a nickname immediately. Instead of Farley Mowat, I became known as Hardly Know-it.

CALLWOOD: Were you crushed by this as a fledgling writer?

MOWAT: I didn't love it, but what it did was stimulate me to greater excesses in my attitudes *(laughs)*. Many people supported me. Scott Young, who wrote for *Saturday Night* at the time, wrote a very supportive article.

CALLWOOD: You've been friends ever since.

MOWAT: Yes.

CALLWOOD: Tweedsmuir wrote that you were another Robert Louis Stevenson. I don't know how you felt about that, but you got some good reviews for that book.

MOWAT: Yes, but I wasn't another Robert Louis Stevenson. I like his work, but I'm certainly not him. You know, I've been called many things by people in authority, and I have long since learned to pay very little attention to what they say about me. What I listen to is what individual human beings who read my books say to me. I may meet someone in a train station who will look at me and say, "I sure liked that last book of yours. It opened my eyes." Or I may get a letter from a kid living in British Columbia saying, "I didn't like books until I read one of your books. Now I read." That is the sort of thing that counts.

CALLWOOD: Yeah, that's great.

MOWAT: You know this yourself. You've had the same experience. You've been belaboured by the establishment more than I have actually.

CALLWOOD: No *(laughs)*.

MOWAT: Well, you have, and you know how rewarding it is when an individual expresses pleasure or gratitude for what you've done.

CALLWOOD: You orginally wrote the pieces that eventually became *People of the Deer* in shorter versions for magazines. There is a story that just before Christmas, when you were on the point of starving, you heard from our agent Max Wilkinson. Is that a true story, or is it apocryphal?

MOWAT: It's a true story. I mean like all my stories it has a grain of truth in it *(laughs)*. You know my famous phrase, "Never let the facts interfere with the truth."

CALLWOOD: Did you make that up?

MOWAT: I made that up. I want everybody to know this because that is my one aphorism.

CALLWOOD: Okay *(laughs)*.

MOWAT: It may last forever. Getting back to your original question, what had happened was that I had written a short story called "Eskimo Spring," which was the essence of the terrible starvation epic that these people had endured the spring that I had arrived. I tried to get the story published in Canada. I sent it to *Maclean's* first. W. O. Mitchell was then the editor.

CALLWOOD: The fiction editor.

MOWAT: He was the fiction editor, but he chose the magazine pieces.

CALLWOOD: Oh, did he?

MOWAT: Yes. He dropped me a note saying that he wanted to discuss this piece with me in person. So I drove down from Palgrave in my little Jeep. I was full of anticipation, of course. *Maclean's* was going to buy this piece, I was sure. All W. O. Mitchell, who was a giant in my eyes, was going to do was tell me he'd like some editorial changes. So I finally arrived in his office — I wearing shorts and a bush shirt as I remember. I didn't look particularly prepossessing. He was sitting behind his desk and he looked up at me and said "Sit down, Mr. Mowat." I sat down, and he went on doing what he was doing for a couple of minutes, which was fair enough. Then he looked up and said, "I read your piece and we can't use it." My heart sank and the bottom fell out. Why had he brought me 40 miles to tell me he couldn't use it? He then added, "But I can give you some very good advice for your future as a young writer in this country. My

advice is that you write boy-meets-girl stories with a happy ending. They should be 5,000 words long." With that I crawled back
out into my Jeep and drove back to Palgrave. Bill gets pissed off
at me telling his story. But in point of fact he probably didn't
have much of an alternative. In those days the market was largely restricted to formula stuff. So he was suggesting to me that if I
followed this formula, I could make a living as a writer. I'm sure
that he didn't intend me to spend the rest of my life doing that. I
think his advice was well-intended. I don't hold any grudge.

CALLWOOD: You still haven't taken his advice. You have not
written one single boy-meets-girl story with a happy ending in
your whole life *(laughs)*.

MOWAT: That's his fault. Now, if that incident hadn't happened, I'd be writing advice for the lovelorn. I'd be writing
romance stories . . .

CALLWOOD: Sure you would.

MOWAT: . . . and I'd be a rich man.

CALLWOOD: Unlike this poverty-stricken individual before me
(laughs).

MOWAT: Ah, it's terrible to be poverty-stricken.

CALLWOOD: I'd like to talk now about your experiences in
World War II. Like so many teenagers, you joined the Army
in the late, lamented war. You were 19 years old, I gather.

MOWAT: Yes.

CALLWOOD: You were part of the Hasty Ps, weren't you?

MOWAT: Yes. The Hasty Ps were the Hastings Prince Edward
Regiment. We were plough jockeys.

CALLWOOD: Yes, infantry. The worst.

MOWAT: Well, I don't know. We didn't think so. As far as we
were concerned, we were top of the line.

CALLWOOD: No, I mean you had the worst job.

MOWAT: Yes. It was a rough business.

CALLWOOD: And you fought up through Italy with that gang.

MOWAT: Yes. We landed in Sicily in July of 1943 and fought our way through Sicily and then Italy. Then, at the beginning of 1945, they transferred us to the northwest European theatre, and we finished the war in Holland.

CALLWOOD: The Battle of Scheldt, too? Did you do that?

MOWAT: No, we didn't get into that.

CALLWOOD: That was a nasty piece.

MOWAT: Yes. It was all nasty. The whole bloody thing was nasty.

CALLWOOD: I've never quite believed the "Follow me, men" story about your landing in Sicily. Is it true?

MOWAT: Unfortunately, it is absolutely true *(laughs)*. It's not only true, it's factual.

CALLWOOD: All right *(laughs)*. Tell us the story.

MOWAT: Well, we were coming ashore in the assault wave on the Pachino [peninsula] on this beautiful summer morning. Behind us the whole sky was livid with the explosions from an enormous fleet of monitors and battleships shelling the beaches. My belly was filled with fear. I was absolutely trembling internally and I was also getting seasick. Our little cockleshell of a landing craft was rocking back and forth.

CALLWOOD: This was your first time in action.

MOWAT: Yes, it was. We touch down on the beach, and this is my moment. I am at the bow of this little tin box with 30 men behind me. We are all waiting for the door to go down. Eventually the door goes down with a rush. I don't realize it, but we have hit a sandbar about a hundred yards offshore. But I am beyond thinking about anything like that, so I simply turn to my men and in my high squeaky little voice shout, "Follow me, men!" Clutching my revolver in one hand, I then stride off the end of the ramp of the landing door and go down into nine feet of water *(laughs)*.

CALLWOOD: You're not nine feet tall, Farley.

MOWAT: No, I'm not even nine feel tall with my arm up and a pistol. They couldn't even see my pistol. I was so heavily accoutered with gear — I was carrying all my web equipment and weaponry, and so on — that I went straight down and landed on my feet on the bottom. What do you do in a case like that? I mean by the time I'd taken off all my gear, it would have been too late; I would have drowned. So I walked as rapidly as I could through the water, upright. It couldn't have been nine feet, maybe it was seven.

CALLWOOD: Oh, Farley *(laughs)*!

MOWAT: Anyway soon my tin hat appeared, and then my head. I looked back and there was my platoon of ferocious infantrymen ready to take on the Germany army; the whole bloody lot of them were clustered around the bow of the boat holding each other up, because they were laughing so hard.

CALLWOOD: That's funny stuff *(laughs)*.

MOWAT: I didn't get a medal for it, either.

CALLWOOD: Nothing was funny after that, but that's a very funny story. Is it true that you wrote one of your most famous and beloved books, *The Dog that Wouldn't Be*, in Ortona or some such dreadful place?

MOWAT: Yes. I did so during the second year in Italy when things were really getting desperate.

CALLWOOD: You were in the mountains at this point, weren't you?

MOWAT: We were in the mountains. Well, we were on the east coast, but it was winter and there was mud and snow. It was a slogging match and it was just a question of who was going to kill everybody else — the Germans or us. It was a really bad scene, and I was losing it. My slim hold on sanity was becoming even slimmer. The only way I could survive was by escaping into the past. So I escaped into my childhood. I would write little pieces about my dog Mutt and my childhood in Saskatoon on scraps of paper. Writing preserved my sanity. It enabled me to endure the unendurable somewhat longer.

CALLWOOD: How could you have concentrated with the shelling around you?

MOWAT: It was easy. You'd clutch to your bosom or clutch in your mind anything that would distract you from it. And thinking about the past was a distraction.

CALLWOOD: Is this where you developed your passionate feeling of man's and woman's inhumanity and decided that you wanted no part of that kind of civilization?

MOWAT: I think I subconsciously became aware of what a bad species I belonged to — but not consciously. At that stage the conscious mind was still in control. However, the seeds had been planted. From then on, this growth within me — some people call it a bad cancer — came to dominate me. Actually it's not bad and it's not cancerous. What it was and still is is a true awareness of what kind of an animal we are.

CALLWOOD: We're destructive animals.

MOWAT: Yes. We're not good. Once you understand that, you can do one of two things: You can commit suicide or you can forgive your own kind and yourself because you belong, and try to make amends. I think without making any claims to being a good person or anything else, I've been trying to make amends ever since.

CALLWOOD: The places you've lived speak volumes about you. You've lived in Palgrave, Burgeo, Cape Breton, and Port Hope. You flee from the centres of activity. Someone said — maybe it was you —that you're seeking tranquillity. Is that true?

MOWAT: No, I'm not in search of tranquillity. I just want to escape from the black hole. The black hole, into which mankind is being sucked, is represented by the metropolitan zones. There you have enormous numbers of human beings, all disassociated from tribe, from family, from history and all brought together in one enormous aggregation of distress, apprehension, misery, and greed.

CALLWOOD: They're also alienated from each other.

MOWAT: Yes, and it terrifies me. It's like somebody standing on a prairie and looking at a cyclone. I want to avoid that. I'm not going to go straight into that cyclone. I'm going to run the other way. But it's not looking for tranquillity.

CALLWOOD: When I saw that house that you built yourself at Palgrave on that 10-acre lot where you and Fran first set up housekeeping, I was struck by the fact that even though you were miles from your neighbours you still had to build another little wee house away from the main house. You still needed more privacy.

MOWAT: Well, I subsequently became even more antisocial. Palgrave was 40 miles from Toronto and in those days — that was 1949, 1950 — it was a pretty tranquil part of the world. There were still farmers living there, and everything was pretty peaceful. But after a while hunters started coming out from Toronto. I couldn't tolerate these guys walking onto my property and shooting everything that flew, swam, or crawled. So, first of all I tried shooting back.

CALLWOOD: You didn't!

MOWAT: I didn't shoot at them. I'd shoot over their heads. At the time, I had an automatic army rifle, which would go *brrrrrr*. This worked up to a point, but then I began to get nervous about it. I thought, maybe I'll hit one of these guys and then I'll be in trouble. So I went up to Orangeville to the local paper, the *Orangeville Banner*, and had them print me some cardboard signs, which read: Danger. Radiation Hazard to Unprotected Personnel. Keewatin Research Authority. I put these up all over the property. Well, instantly, nobody came near the place. The milkman wouldn't come near, the breadman wouldn't, the meter reader wouldn't come in. Nobody would, and property values plunged all around me. My neighbours couldn't sell their land *(laughs)*. This went on for a while, so I had peace and quiet. Nobody bothered me. But then one day a big black car drove into my little gravel driveway. Out of it came three guys in suits. I looked at them and I could smell bureaucrat. I thought, uh-oh, this is trouble. I walked over to them — I'd been working in the garden, so I was half-naked and sweaty — and I said, "What can I do for you guys?" They said, "Do you have a source of nuclear power here or a nuclear reactor?" I said, "No, I don't." "What do those signs mean then?" they asked. I said, "Well, you are engineers?" to which they replied yes. "University graduates?" I queried further. "Yes," they replied. "Well, if you'd spent less time concentrating on engineering and more on the English language, you'd be able to understand those signs," I shot back. They said, "What the hell do you mean?" I said, "Well, all they mean is that if you come on my property naked on a sunny day you'll get sunburned: Danger. Radiation Hazard to Unprotected Personnel." They were very angry. They were going to take me to court for committing mischief or being a public nuisance or something like that. Anyway the signs gave me tranquillity for a while.

CALLWOOD: And a good laugh *(laughs)*!

MOWAT: Yes.

CALLWOOD: The reason you had that automatic rifle you used to chase away intruders was that you came home from World War II with enough stuff to outfit the army of the Congo.

MOWAT: Yes, well, that wasn't intentional. Nothing's intentional in my life. One thing leads to another. What happened was at the end of the war I was foolishly and incorrectly convinced that we were going to have to fight another war with the Russians, with the Communists. The propaganda was that we were going to have to fight them and that the Red Menace was going to clobber us. Because I was a technical intelligence officer at the end of the war, I knew that piece-for-piece German equipment was infinitely superior to ours technically. So I took it on myself to make a collection of German equipment.

CALLWOOD: So that you'd be ready for World War III?

MOWAT: So that we in the West would be, so Canada would be.

CALLWOOD: Oh, these were going to be prototypes.

MOWAT: Some of them were. Oh, wait until I tell you about some of the stuff we brought back. It's a long story, which I've told in short form in the letters in *My Father's Son*. Anyway, I finished up with a buckshee unit, that is, an illegal unit. We called ourselves the First Canadian War Museum Collection Team. We invented the name and we had rubber stamps made with the name on it so we could do all the proper military things.

CALLWOOD: Collection team *(laughs)*!

MOWAT: Yes, and I chartered a Dutch liberty ship in Brussels.

CALLWOOD: You were the rank of captain, weren't you?

MOWAT: Yes. That's how I could get away with it. If I'd been any higher rank, people would have suspected there was something wrong. But nobody suspected a mere captain. They assumed that I was acting under orders. I brought back 750 tons of German equipment [by ship]. One of the items we stole was a V-2 rocket. At that time the British, the Russians, and the Americans had agreed no smaller countries would be allowed access to German rocketry. So we stole this thing, dragged it back into our hideout in Brussels, painted it blue, put a wooden conning tower on it, and packed it off to the one-man submarine *(laughs)*.

CALLWOOD: When you got to Canada with this, were you greeted warmly by customs?

MOWAT: Well, customs had nothing to do with it. This was a military shipment. But I was not greeted warmly by National Defence. National Defence headquarters nearly had conniptions.

CALLWOOD: But you'd been doing this out of patriotic duty.

MOWAT: Yeah, for the best of all reasons. There was quite a to-do when I got back. But again, because I was a captain, nobody thought of pinning the blame on me. There was the question of a $75,000 shipping bill for chartering this boat.

CALLWOOD: That would be like a million dollars now.

MOWAT: Exactly. They kept me on in Ottawa for six months on staff pay while they tried to find out who had authorized this and how the whole thing had come about.

CALLWOOD: Did they find out it was you *(laughs)*?

MOWAT: They never did. They finally gave me my discharge and said, "Go away. We don't want to see you again."

CALLWOOD: Well, that leads us straight into the RCMP collecting data on you because of your dangerous Communist leanings. What is your status vis à vis the United States at this moment, Farley?

MOWAT: I've been taken off the black book. Me and Bertrand Russell and several other more prominent people than myself who were excluded. We formed a little group called the Excludees Incorporated and felt very proud of ourselves.

CALLWOOD: You must have had lots of meetings.

MOWAT: Yes, and they were pretty alcoholic. But anyway the Senate, or whatever they call it in the United States — we'd better learn the terminology because they're going to be running us internally pretty soon — finally passed a bill two years ago to the effect that those people who had been excluded for political sympathies that were not pro-American could now be admitted. But I will not go back to the United States. I won't set foot there until they meet my minimum requirement, which I stated at the time they excluded me. I said that I would not cross the border until they sent Air Force I to salute me or a letter of apology from whoever happens to be president of their dictatorship.

CALLWOOD: You might just get that from Clinton. He seems to have a sense of wit about him. That would disappoint you.

MOWAT: Well, he might give me a letter, but I don't think he's going to send Air Force I. Wouldn't it be funny if he did?

CALLWOOD: It'd be a hoot.

MOWAT: Yeah. I'd like to see it try and land at my place in Cape Breton *(laughs)*.

CALLWOOD: Which brings us to all the places that you have fled to in your search for paradise. Have you found it yet?

MOWAT: No. There's no such place, of course. But I tell you what I have found in my part of Cape Breton. I've found acceptance on a level that I had not encountered anywhere else in Canada, except in the High North. The community in which I live is called River Bourgeois — imagine me living in a place called River Bourgeois. Despite its rather hoity-toity name, it is more accepting, more tolerant of outsiders than any other place I've ever been. And that makes it heaven on earth for me.

CALLWOOD: When you went to Burgeo in Newfoundland you thought that, too.

MOWAT: I thought that, too, but then, of course, what happened was that I dirtied my own doorstep in the incident with the whale that came into the lagoon. The locals shot at it and eventually killed it. Of course, I took the side of the whale and criticized their actions, which alienated everybody in town. I held them up to ridicule to the outer world, which was a terrible thing to do. I didn't do it deliberately, but that's the way things ended. I muddied the waters there so I had to get out.

CALLWOOD: That was a heartbreaking time.

MOWAT: It was indeed.

CALLWOOD: You've glossed over that incident, but it really must have been heartbreaking on both sides. The locals were horrified by what you did, but they really did shoot at that whale.

MOWAT: A small group of degenerates in the community did. There will always be people like that. These were actually people who'd become degenerates by going to Ontario to work and then come back. If they'd never gone, they'd have been all right. However, these are the people who caused the trouble and killed a whale. The majority of the community had nothing to do with it and even sympathized with my attempts to save the whale. But when the world press got hold of the story and everybody dumped on Burgeo, they drew together.

CALLWOOD: People do.

MOWAT: Yes, of course. They were in pain because I'd hurt them.

CALLWOOD: You and Claire had lived there for six to eight years.

MOWAT: Yes.

CALLWOOD: Not to be welcome there must have been saddening.

MOWAT: Yes it was, but one recovers from these things.

CALLWOOD: Margaret Atwood once said that if *Moby Dick* had been written by a Canadian it would have been written from the point of view of the whale. So you were being quintessentially Canadian in choosing the whale's side.

MOWAT: Yes, I suppose so.

CALLWOOD: After leaving Burgeo, you moved to Port Hope, where you later found out that you were next to a nuclear power plant, didn't you?

MOWAT: Well, no. I knew about the Eldorado plant in Port Hope before we moved there. It has been there since the days when they discovered radium in the 1930s. People were getting pitchblende from Great Slave Lake and bringing it down to Port Hope to refine it. They refined it in an old shed down at the waterfront. Out of this grew the uranium industry. I don't know how many people are aware of this, but the uranium for both Hiroshima and Nagasaki came from Port Hope.

CALLWOOD: Oh, I hate to hear that.

MOWAT: It's a nice thought.

CALLWOOD: And that's the place you picked, this pretty town.

MOWAT: Yes, that pretty town. As I said, I knew about the Eldorado plant. But my mother lived in Port Hope. At that time my father actually lived there, too. And it was as close to Toronto as I dared go. It was 60 miles from Toronto, so we stayed there. It's not so bad. Well, it's pretty bad, but there is always a bright spot.

CALLWOOD: What's the bright spot?

MOWAT: Well, our ancestors used to go to Baden-Baden in Germany to drink the radioactive waters, because they believed it would restore their flagging vigour.

CALLWOOD: How are you doing?

MOWAT: I'm feeling pretty vigorous, kid, pretty vigorous!

CALLWOOD: There'll be a stampede to Port Hope tomorrow.

MOWAT: Real estate values in Port Hope will soar, and I will be thanked for it.

CALLWOOD: Farley, in your house in Port Hope, the number of books you've written and the translations of them virtually form a wall. How many books are there? Thirty-five?

MOWAT: Thirty-three, I think. I can only count to 30. Beyond that it's guesswork.

CALLWOOD: You're very popular in Russia, or you used to be.

MOWAT: I used to be.

CALLWOOD: Weren't your royalties frozen in Russia?

MOWAT: That is the operative phrase. They were frozen in Siberia, deep frozen, yes *(laughs)*.

CALLWOOD: Wasn't the upshot that you got a free boat ride to Russia?

MOWAT: That's right. I did. The Russians were not members of the International Copyright Association. This was not because they didn't want to be, they tried. But the Americans wouldn't let them in. So as a result they didn't pay royalties the same way we do. They just kept the money there. If you wanted it, you had to go to get it. So Claire and I took the opportunity to go over there in 1966. We had a marvellous trip on a Russian passenger ship. It was the first voyage that she had made carrying passengers from the West, and the whole thing was uproarious. Everybody, including the captain, ended up in the swimming pool at three o'clock in the morning drinking vodka. I think we were swimming in vodka, actually. It was a great trip.

CALLWOOD: Was this *The Pushkin*?

MOWAT: Yes, *The Alexander Pushkin*.

CALLWOOD: Did you have lots of caviar?

MOWAT: Yes. Oh, it was a great trip. We travelled through Siberia, and I was so interested in what we saw that I wrote a book about that called *Sibir*.

CALLWOOD: Were you responsible for changing Russian policy about wolves?

MOWAT: The Russians tell me I was. They published *Never Cry Wolf* there, although they had trouble with the translation. *Never Cry Wolf* is a special phrase in English. It's an idiom that doesn't exist in Russian. So they published the book as *Wolves, Please Don't Cry.*

CALLWOOD: Oh, come on *(laughs)*!

MOWAT: They did, so help me. The book was so successful that the Russian conservation authorities did pull back on wolf control. I don't know whether the situation remains the same under the new capitalist regime in Moscow or the dictatorship or whatever you want to call it. But they'll be out there shooting wolves again very shortly, not doubt.

CALLWOOD: If there's any money in it.

MOWAT: Exactly.

CALLWOOD: Of all the environmental books you've written, which do you think contributed to setting environmental policy on a more humane course?

MOWAT: I don't know. I would hope *Sea of Slaughter* was the most effective. But I don't think that's the case because that book is such a dreadful compendium of the terrible things we have done that most people can't read it.

CALLWOOD: It's heartbreaking.

MOWAT: They read a chapter and then stop. It took me five years to write it. Three times I stopped; I couldn't go on with it. I had to put it aside. And three times I came back to it and said to myself, by God I'll finish it if it kills me. It certainly is the most damning indictment of mankind's crimes against nature that I've ever written. But whether it was the most effective book, I don't know. Maybe *Never Cry Wolf* was, because kids still write to me to tell me how it changed their feelings about wolves, and in so doing changed their feeling about nonhuman life.

CALLWOOD: It's a start, isn't it?

MOWAT: Yes. I think it may have been fairly influential.

CALLWOOD: Well *Sea of Slaughter* was certainly prophetic, because five years after it came out people began to lament the decline of the cod population and the disappearance of other species from the ocean.

MOWAT: You know, to be a prophet in your own land is to be a prophet without honour or without recognition, and that suits me. However, it doesn't give me any sense of satisfaction to know that five years after I told them that we were overfishing the ocean and that the cod were going they realize this is true. There's no satisfaction in being right. It's just a fact that this is what happened. I read a terrible story about a related incident in yesterday's paper. The story was from St. John's, Newfoundland, and it revealed that the International Fund for Animal Welfare has just discovered from leaked documents that the Newfoundland government has licensed the shipment of 60,000 seal penises from Newfoundland to Asia, where they will be sold as aphrodisiacs. They are planning to slaughter 60,000 harp seals on the ice for their penises. That is almost the last straw. You know the seal slaughter has been stopped. Everybody now understands that it was not the seals that were destroying the fishery, but rather us. So now they're going to go after the seals as aphrodisiacs for Asians. If they do this, so help me, God, I think I'll resign from the human race.

CALLWOOD: You've been threatening to resign for a long time.

MOWAT: Yes *(laughs)*.

CALLWOOD: You hopped a continent for another species that fascinates me, the gorilla. How did that movie star, Sigourney Weaver, end up on your doorstep? I never managed to put that story together.

MOWAT: Like all my stories, it's a convoluted one that doesn't make much sense. It just happened. I'd written a book about Diane Fossey. Actually she used me to write a book about her. That's what happened with that one. I lost control in the first 15 pages and she took over. Later the movie was made, not from my book but from Fossey's own book, *Gorillas in the Mist*. However, Sigourney Weaver had read my book. She was apparently very intrigued by the character of Diane Fossey, whom she was going to play. So she showed up on my bloody doorstep in Port Hope one day. A great limousine drove up to the door, and Claire, who was with me, said, "What's that? Did we order a limo?" And I said, "No, we don't order limos. Is there one out there?" She replied in the affirmative. So I went out and there was this beautiful tall woman. I gazed up at her and knew she looked familiar. She introduced herself and said she'd like to talk about Diane Fossey. We talked and I showed her Diane Fossey's journals. She went off to a corner of our living room and read these journals for an hour or so. Then she took us out for dinner, and that was it. End of story.

CALLWOOD: Did you see *Gorillas in the Mist* when it was released?

MOWAT: Yes.

CALLWOOD: Did you think that was Diane Fossey?

MOWAT: I thought the gorillas were terrific.

CALLWOOD: Weren't they wonderful?

MOWAT: Mm-hmm.

CALLWOOD: You're not going to comment on Sigourney Weaver who was right in your living room?

MOWAT: Well, she did all right, I guess, within the limits that were imposed upon her by Hollywood.

CALLWOOD: I'd like to ask you a different kind of question, if I may. Farley, what is the meaning of life?

MOWAT: I don't know what the meaning of it is. I know what the nature of it is. The nature of it is continuity and survival. Everything that we do and everything that we are is dedicated to the ongoing flow of this substance, this condition we call life. Maybe there is no meaning. Anyway, I don't concern myself with meaning. Meaning is a rational concept. As I grow older, I am less and less delighted by the rational approach. I am less and less delighted by intellect. I suspect that it's the rational, intellectual capacity in man that's going to destroy him. I'm much more concerned with feelings and emotions. This is, I think, where salvation might lie.

CALLWOOD: You've made yourself available to a lot of people who are fighting to protect the environment. You're in with the antilogging people in B.C., aren't you?

MOWAT: Yeah, but I don't extend myself that far.

CALLWOOD: Elizabeth May said you were going to ride the train.

MOWAT: I did, from Kingston to Toronto (laughs). I was very damn careful not to ride it as far as Victoria because I might have gotten arrested. The situation I'm in now is that I am behind the lines, cheering on the troops. I'm no longer up there at the front.

CALLWOOD: You do more than that. You write books and you put in a penny or two.

MOWAT: Well, from here on in, I'll tell you what I'm going to do. In fact, I've already done it with my current book. I am writing to give pleasure to myself as well as others. My current book is *Born Naked*, which is about my first 16 years upon this benighted planet — from conception up to my 16th birthday.

CALLWOOD: We all know you were conceived in a canoe. It must have been a very tippy way to do it.

MOWAT: (laughs) That's my father's story. My mother's story differs.

CALLWOOD: She ought to know. I would question your father.

MOWAT: I told that story about the green canoe for years. However, one day I asked my mother if it really happened that way.

She must have had an extra glass of sherry that day because normally she wouldn't talk about things like this. She said, "Actually it was in the horse barns at the Canadian National Exhibition." I said, "What, mother?" She said, "Well, we went to the Ex and it started to rain. Angus hadn't brought an umbrella, so we went into the barns to get out from under the rain. There was nobody in there but those horses and all that straw. . . ."

CALLWOOD: Do you like that story better?

MOWAT: No. It doesn't fit.

CALLWOOD: Being born in the stables seems not bad to me.

MOWAT: I don't like it. It makes me think of our famous poet Irving Layton, who sometimes says that he's the reincarnation of Christ. I don't want to get into that league. The competition is too tough. Besides, I prefer canoes to horses and barns. So that's where I say I was conceived *(laughs)*.

CALLWOOD: *(laughs)* You ought to know. After all, you were right there. Your childhood was unusual in that you were surrounded by animals and birds, but there weren't many people in your life.

MOWAT: Well, there weren't a lot of people in my life. For one thing I was sort of outside the pale. I was a little sawed-off character. I always looked three years younger than I was, so I couldn't compete with children my own age.

CALLWOOD: You were smart as hell, though.

MOWAT: Yes. For another thing, we were moving all the time. As a result I never really became established anywhere. We were an early part of the peripatetic generation. Moreover, my curiosity about my fellow human beings was easily satisfied. I could figure them out; I knew what was going on; I could see what they were doing. But my curiosity about the nonhuman forms of life around me was enormous because I didn't understand them. They were different. So I was drawn to them.

CALLWOOD: You weren't just drawn to something adorable like a cat or a dog. You found creatures like rattlesnakes interesting.

MOWAT: Yes. I had a rattlesnake in my bureau drawer for a while in Saskatoon. It was a very neat symbiotic arrangement: I had the rattlesnake in the middle drawer; in the top drawer, I had white mice so that the feeding procedures were quite simple *(laughs)*.

CALLWOOD: Oh, Farley. You fed it live mice?

MOWAT: Well I averted my eyes.

CALLWOOD: Well, that was tasteful *(laughs)*. What other kinds of animals did you have?

MOWAT: Actually, anything you can name at one time or another that was available to a kid.

CALLWOOD: What purpose did these odd critters serve in your life?

MOWAT: They gave me comfort. Somehow they alleviated my sense of aloneness. They established a connection for me with life *en masse*, I guess you could say. They probably made it possible for me to survive the unendurable in many cases, and I've been paying them back for it ever since.

CALLWOOD: I find life is immensely sad.

MOWAT: Well, you have experienced a great deal of sadness.

CALLWOOD: I think life is sad for most people.

MOWAT: Yes, it can be indeed. But an awful lot of solace is available to us if we choose to open ourselves up to nonhuman animals. They don't seem to be oppressed as we are by ongoing sadness, by apprehension, by enormous anxieties, by all the distress that afflicts us. They don't seem to be, and I don't really think they are. They can give to us a sense of belonging, a sense of merit, a sense of being viable and valid. That's why I love them.

CALLWOOD: You can get that from a wolf?

MOWAT: Yes.

CALLWOOD: You've made me love wolves.

MOWAT: I can get that feeling from almost any animal. For instance, I felt very comfortable with that little cat that was sitting on my lap a while ago, that poor little skinny thing, full of fleas, and so on. In fact, I probably related better to the cat than I do to most of the crew here, who probably have fleas, too *(laughs)*.

CALLWOOD: You're really uncomfortable with most people aren't you, Farley?

MOWAT: I'm uncomfortable with a lot of people. That's why my protective mechanism goes up and why all my life I've carried this cardboard cutout of myself — you know, Farley Mowat the drinker, Farley Mowat the pseudo-Scot. That's a protective mechanism.

CALLWOOD: Do you think you fool people?

MOWAT: Well, I fool some people. But that doesn't matter. What matters is that I feel protected by the cutout.

CALLWOOD: You come in and play Farley Mowat and then you can stay behind the screen.

MOWAT: Yes.

CALLWOOD: You're a watcher, aren't you?

MOWAT: Yes, I'm an observer, which I think any storyteller must be. You see, I'm essentially a storyteller.

CALLWOOD: Yes, you are.

MOWAT: I am not an artist, I don't consider myself a literary person. I'm a storyteller in the ancient tradition, and you become a storyteller by watching.

CALLWOOD: Didn't you once say to me that we're good hacks?

MOWAT: As writers?

CALLWOOD: Yes.

MOWAT: Well, I may have said that, but if so, I would qualify it. I'd say we're good hacks in sort of a gentle tone of voice.

CALLWOOD: I think you did use that tone. Storytellers are vitally important.

MOWAT: Exactly. Without us the human race would have disintegrated long ago.

CALLWOOD: It comes back to what you said about continuity, doesn't it?

MOWAT: Yes.

CALLWOOD: Continuity is what matters.

MOWAT: Mm-hmm.

CALLWOOD: We've been friends for 40 years.

MOWAT: That's right, and we will be for another 40.

CALLWOOD: Absolutely.

Karen Kain

$\mathcal{P}$eople who saw the interview with Karen Kain always mention the kitten who slept on her lap throughout, while she stroked its tiny back with mesmerizing tenderness. They comment most especially on how open she was. The ballerina's posture is willowy and elegant, leading many to assume that Karen must be distant and secretive, but instead she is unfailingly warm and candid.

Canada has had several outstanding dancers in recent years, but Karen Kain's movements have a purity that causes audiences to hold their breath in awe. She is simply inspiring in the great classical ballets. She has danced her last *Sleeping Beauty*, alas, but did it perfectly in May 1994 in the sweltering heart of Israel on an open-air stage not meant for dance.

The final performance capped more than 20 years in that most demanding ballet. While remaining a loyal member of the National Ballet of Canada, she has danced with every major company in the world and with some of the most dramatic male dancers in the business — Canada's Frank Augustyn, notably, but also the flamboyant Russian Rudolf Nureyev, who was enchanted by her and took her dancing all over the world. He said of her that she possesses "the special radiance that lights up the whole stage."

She's a choreographer's dream because she will work until she drops to perfect the movements and the feeling. Roland Petit and Glen Tetley, among others, created works for her. Anna Kisselgoff, respected dance critic for the *New York Times*, called her "simply the best female dancer on stage."

Karen Kain was born in Hamilton in 1951 and was given the careful upbringing that tends to result in stable, optimistic, self-disciplined people. She once said that her ambition was to be a nice person all her life. She has succeeded so well in that endeavour that one artistic director told her she would never be a great ballerina because she wasn't bitchy enough.

Karen appears frequently in the annual benefit, Dancers for Life, which raises money for the AIDS Committee of Toronto, but her charity-of-choice in recent years has been Toronto's Dancer Transition Centre, a resource centre that assists dancers to adjust to life after they can dance no more. Dancers push their bodies as hard as do hockey players, and retirement is hazardous to their emotional and financial well-being. Dancers have always known that postcareer years can be full of poverty and pain, but Karen Kain was among the first in this country to try to help.

She has been married since 1983 to actor Ross Petty and they live in suburban Toronto with a cat.

When we finished the interview, Karen gently transferred the sleepy kitten to a pillow. She had just left the coach house when someone remembered that she had stipulated two questions I should not ask. As it turned out, I hadn't asked either of them. Piece of luck.

CALLWOOD: When I sit in the audience watching you perform, it seems to me you reach perfection. I've often wondered if dance is one of the few things in life where there is a moment when you know that it can't be done any better. Have you ever had a moment like that?

KAIN: Maybe a second.

CALLWOOD: Oh, come on.

KAIN: Really.

CALLWOOD: Aren't there times when you finish a movement and think, I did that just as well as it could be done?

KAIN: Sometimes I have a movement like that where I know I couldn't do it any better. I know that I practised and practised and yet it still happened when I wanted it to happen, so I'm really happy. But then there will be another movement that I'll feel I didn't do as well as I wanted to. I don't think I've ever been through an entire performance where I had every movement the way I knew I could do it. However, I have had those seconds and they are what make me keep working because I want more of those seconds to happen. I want them to occur not just in the studio when I'm by myself but also under the pressure of performing for all those people who've paid a lot of money and who expect a certain level of performance.

CALLWOOD: So when people are on their feet and they're throwing flowers at you, you're thinking, I didn't quite get that right?

KAIN: Oh, I'm always very happy when the audience responds that way because I know they've enjoyed what they've seen. However, most of the time I'm thinking, well, this part was good, but I didn't get that, even though I worked so hard. Usually there's some disappointment involved for me.

CALLWOOD: It's like high board diving where the diver can do a certain dive over and over again when he's on his own but doesn't quite manage to do it under the pressure of a competition.

KAIN: One little miscalculation, one fraction of a second of loss of concentration and it isn't what it could be. Nobody knows except you and the person who's worked with you in the studio and, perhaps, your partner. Maybe your timing hasn't been as good as you both know it could be and you weren't quite together. Nervousness can do that to you. It can really affect your concentration.

CALLWOOD: Thirteen choreographers, I believe, have done original works just for you. How do you learn a whole dance? What's the process?

KAIN: It depends on the person you're working with. Sometimes it's a very collaborative affair and that's what I enjoy. But often with some of the great choreographers, they have everything in their mind. They know exactly what they want from you, and they don't really want your contribution, thank you very much. I mean they know you're capable. They let you believe that you're capable of achieving what they see in their mind, but they will not allow you to do something the way you feel it should be done. It's their way. That is a lot more difficult for me but just as rewarding in the end, because I end up discovering things by fighting my own natural instincts and trying to find what they want.

CALLWOOD: So they've written a piece with you in mind. They want you to perform it, so they're thinking of what you can do. You're going to show their piece off, and it's going to show you off.

KAIN: But sometimes they want to see something different from what you've done before, which is a challenge for them and a challenge for me. I enjoy that, too.

CALLWOOD: But then how do you learn? Where do you start with the steps? Is that where using the mirror comes in?

KAIN: I don't use the mirror much. It's funny. I know that everyone thinks of the dancer and the mirror. I use the mirror when I'm working in my training to correct myself and to look at my placement, because things never look the way they feel. But I don't have the mirror when I'm actually rehearsing on the stage. I find it's impossible to rely on a mirror to find where you should be. You need to feel it, and you don't feel if you're look-ing in the mirror and your concentration is not where it should be. So I don't use it often. With the choreographer sometimes we start by talking. He will explain to me what he's trying to achieve. Sometimes they don't give me much at all. Then I wait until it becomes clear in the process.

CALLWOOD: Do they talk about the emotion of the dance or the techniques?

KAIN: I find if we talk about a character I begin to understand who they see as this character. Then I start to understand how to move, how to think, and how to feel. Therefore I begin to move more in the way they might want me to move. So talking helps them and it helps me. I'm always happy when people start from the inside out because I think that's where dancing should come from.

CALLWOOD: Is it true that young dancers are more interested in conquering the technique and that as they mature they start using their feelings as well? Is the latter the stage you're at? The critics seem to think that's the case.

KAIN: Yes, I think so. I think I concentrated very much on the technique when I was younger. I could not think about the emotional part of it because I didn't believe that my technique would hold up if I let my concentration go to something else in the dancing. Now I believe the emotional part is more important, so I have to concentrate on both at the same time. I wish I'd started sooner, but I wasn't guided that way. I was only guided to work on my technique. Of course, that was because my technique needed improvement. But I figure at this point my technique is always going to be lacking. So I now concentrate on what appeals to me and what I think is important.

CALLWOOD: So you've got two voices in your head when you're dancing. One watches your technique and the other one watches the performer, the actor.

KAIN: I find the thing that holds everything together and centres everything for me while I'm dancing, no matter what voice is giving me what directions, is the music and the story. Not all ballets have a story, but they all have music, and that is the thing that tells me everything. It gives me coordination; it gives me the feeling of the step; it gives me the impetus for the technique; it gives me everything. That's what saves me from terrible stage fright. I just focus my concentration completely on the music and on my partner or whoever I'm dancing with.

CALLWOOD: Do you rely on motor memory for your steps or do you think ahead of your steps?

KAIN: It depends on how familiar I am with the dance and how much rehearsal time we've had. Usually we've rehearsed so much that you could turn on the music and my muscles would remember the choreography right away. Sometimes sequences are so complicated that no matter how many times I go over them, I still have to be very aware of the sequence, especially if I'm doing something to very contemporary music. I did a 17-minute solo, which Eliot Feld choreographed in New York.

CALLWOOD: Oh, 17 minutes is a long time.

KAIN: Seventeen minutes required incredible stamina but also incredible concentration because Feld used Steve Reich music, which was very repetitive so that you didn't know exactly where you were in the music. As a result, I had to count. It was almost like doing math and dancing at the same time.

CALLWOOD: Tap dancers count.

KAIN: Yes, and I hate doing that. I hated doing that, but it was the only way that I could be sure of where I was in the music. It wasn't just counting in sixes, it was counting in 11 and 13 and then 18 and then a couple of sixes. If I lost it anywhere, there were so few clues. Fortunately, I never did lose it. It was very satisfying in a different way for me.

CALLWOOD: That's a scary thing to have to do.

KAIN: Yes, it was scary but again it made me concentrate intensely.

CALLWOOD: So much of your dancing is with a partner. When the partnership works well, you can see how erotic ballet really is. Yet finding the right partner must be difficult for someone who's maturing and needs someone as good as she is. That can't be an easy quest.

KAIN: It's not an easy quest. I suppose it's the same for anyone who's an actor or actress. However, if you're a professional, you do your best even if you don't feel any terrific chemistry with your partner. Certainly I've been spoiled in my career because I've had wonderful chemistry with certain partners. So when I don't have that, I'm very very conscious of it. I don't feel that it helps me do my best, but I am professional enough that I can get past it.

CALLWOOD: Well, first of all you need a rather tall partner, because you're five feet seven. When you're on your toes, you must be very tall.

KAIN: I'm at least six feet tall then.

CALLWOOD: Are you really? That means you need a six-foot-tall man since the man dances flatfooted. Frank Augustyn and Rudolf Nureyev are your two most famous partners, and they're not huge.

KAIN: No, they're not. Neither of them is tall, but fortunately they both had enough charisma to make up for their lack of height *(laughs)*.

CALLWOOD: I once saw Nureyev on a plane from Toronto to New York. He was going back there after a performance. I thought he was a construction worker or something, because he had such a muscular body. It wasn't until he put on his full-length black mink coat that it dawned on me who he was.

KAIN: Construction workers don't usually dress like that.

CALLWOOD: No, they don't. But he seems to me to be a fire-plug-shaped guy rather than a really tall dancer. However, he looks strong.

KAIN: Yes, I think he's only five nine. He's amazingly strong, though, as is Frank Augustyn. I mean they have a kind of wiry strength. But they look incredibly powerful on stage. When people would meet Frank at receptions, they wouldn't believe it was him because he's so slight.

CALLWOOD: He's also a mild-mannered man.

KAIN: Yes. Rudolf is not so mild-mannered.

CALLWOOD: The story is that he bullied you when you were a very young dancer.

KAIN: He did bully me, but in the best way. It was his way of showing affection, and he made it very clear that he considered me special and wanted to help me. It was fantastic. I mean you can't imagine. I was 21 years old when I was dancing with him. His way of bullying me would be to add rehearsals for me. He would work with me alone and give me 10,000 corrections, but at the same time he would encourage me.

CALLWOOD: He said you were the best Bluebird anyone ever was.

KAIN: Oh, I don't know if he said that. But I just blossomed, as you do when someone you admire so much believes in you.

CALLWOOD: Especially when he's someone the world admires.

KAIN: Exactly. It was an incredible experience for me. He was also wonderful with the rest of the company. During every performance, he would stand in the wings between his entrances, or as he was warming up for his big entrance, and encourage us and shout corrections at us. Every second was important to him on the stage. He treated the stage as if it were a sacred place. As he got older, sometimes he would disappoint me when he didn't treat the stage that way. But I think I can imagine the kind of physical pain he must have had.

CALLWOOD: You once said that what's important for a woman dancing is her partner's hands, the strength in the hands and the placement.

KAIN: It's strength, it's all of those things, but it's also an instinctive feel for the rhythm of the woman he's partnering. The man has to feel your musicality and understand your preparations. Maybe it's the same thing that they have to have when they're playing basketball. Their reactions have to be incredibly sharp to be able to save a very fast turn before anyone notices that it's starting to go off its equilibrium. This is just a certain kind of coordination. You can learn some of it, but much of it is simply a gift. Some people have it; they're born with it. When you're dancing with a man who has this gift, no matter what you do, he's right there with you; he understands what's happening and fixes things before anybody notices anything is wrong. It's quite a talent, and Frank had that.

CALLWOOD: I always assume that partners are in love with one another because their movements together are so beautiful. It must help if you are in love.

KAIN: I don't think you have to be in love. I think you have to have a rapport and obviously that's easier with some people than with others.

CALLWOOD: You have to care about that person.

KAIN: It helps if you're friends and you're supportive of each other. I've had to dance with a lot of people who try to compete with me. It is a horrible experience when you have a partner who's trying to be seen, who's saying, Look at me. I'm dancing with Karen Kain. That doesn't interest me at all, and it doesn't make for a good performance, either.

CALLWOOD: Don't look at the woman in the tutu, there's me *(laughs)*.

KAIN: Yes, and there are people like that. Frank was always very concerned with making it work with the two of us. He took great pride in the partnering and how well he did it and how good it made both of us look.

CALLWOOD: I don't think there's as much in it for a man, is there?

KAIN: No, because the ballerina is in front. To be a male ballet dancer requires a kind of humility. However, this is not true of contemporary dance.

CALLWOOD: The ballerina gets the best lines.

KAIN: Yes, and people don't know that when a ballerina looks really good it's usually because the person behind her is holding her on her balance or giving her the confidence to really go for steps and not be afraid that the partner isn't going to catch her, isn't going to control the turn or whatever. You can look a lot better with a good partner than with somebody you're a little iffy with. Frank really did that for me.

CALLWOOD: He made you feel safe and then you could do your best.

KAIN: Yes. But also because we rehearsed endlessly and we did so many performances together, we knew exactly how to cope with each other's nerves and all the things that happen in the stress of the moment as opposed to the relaxed atmosphere of the studio. There it doesn't really matter if something doesn't work because you just stop and try it again. But on stage you only have one chance. If something doesn't work, you can't let it affect your concentration and get all freaked out and mess up everything afterwards. It's a big problem.

CALLWOOD: Well, you're both famous for not being prima donnas. That helps a lot, too. I'd like to talk now about your childhood. I ran into your mum one time, and she said, "I never thought Karen was going to be a dancer. She was a chubby little girl." I couldn't imagine you chubby.

KAIN: I was. It was a big problem. Every report card from age 14 on said, "She works very hard, but she has to lose weight."

CALLWOOD: Really? A lot of weight?

KAIN: Yes.

CALLWOOD: There were a lot of you little kids when you were growing up.

KAIN: There were four of us.

CALLWOOD: Who was the boss? You or one of your siblings?

KAIN: Well, I was the oldest, so I always had the control button. I was the one who was sort of in charge because I was older. But you know, I left home fairly young. I left home when I was 11, which was very hard. It was very hard for my mum. I think I only begin to appreciate now how hard it was.

CALLWOOD: This was the National Ballet School. It's not like leaving home with a knapsack on your back.

KAIN: No, not that kind of leaving home. I went into boarding school in order to be a dancer and it was my choice absolutely. I mean it was something I wanted to do.

CALLWOOD: What made you so sure at such a young age?

KAIN: Maybe at 11 I didn't really know what I was getting into. I knew I loved to dance. I did that by myself all the time. I would go downstairs and I would put on recordings and I would dance by myself in the basement. If I wasn't dancing, I would listen to the music and imagine myself dancing to it. However, the selection of music was limited. My dad was very fond of marching bands *(laughs)*. We had a lot of that and Scottish folk songs. But I would listen to anything, you know, just as long as it —

CALLWOOD: And move to it.

KAIN: Yes. Then I started taking ballet lessons. Actually my parents took me to see *Giselle* with Celia Franca. I was seven or eight and that was it. I watched the ballet and thought, this is what I want to do.

CALLWOOD: Lots of little girls fall in love with ballet.

KAIN: Thousands of little girls fall in love with ballet. I started the lessons and I wasn't all that keen on them. But you know that has to do with teachers, and fortunately my mother had read up a little bit about dancing lessons and putting your child in dancing school. My first teacher had one record, Patti Page singing *The Tennessee Waltz*. I would do my half-hour lesson to that. Every week I danced to the same thing over and over.

CALLWOOD: This is how a career starts *(laughs)*?

KAIN: I hear that song every now and then, and it all comes back *(laughs)*. The kind of dance I did was more interpretive dance, but it's a little hard to be interpretive to that music week after week. Then my teacher decided that I needed pointe shoes. My mom had read a little bit about dancing lessons, and she knew that it was very dangerous to put a young child on pointe if they haven't been strengthened properly. So she thought maybe this teacher wasn't the best one for me, and I stopped having those lessons.

CALLWOOD: In time.

KAIN: In time. But fate may have played a role in it, too. We were living in Ancaster at the time, and we went to another teacher there, whose name is Betty Carey. She's still teaching. I took lessons from her every Saturday morning at the Ancaster Community Centre. After I'd been there for a year, she took my mum aside and said, "I really think your daughter is talented. You ought to take her to the National Ballet School and audition her or see what they think." We had never heard of the National Ballet School. They didn't audition across Canada; it wasn't on television. We didn't know anything about it. My mother sat me down and asked me how I felt about this and whether I wanted to pursue it any further. I said I did. So, we went to Toronto, the big city, and I had my audition. I only did a few steps at the barre. Then Betty Oliphant, who was teaching, asked me to wait with my mum after the lesson. She was going to test me in some other way, and have a look at me. So we sat and watched this ballet class. There was a girl who cried all the way through it. My mother was really dismayed by this. She said, "You don't need this. We're going back to Ancaster." But after the lesson, Betty gave me some little things to play out, which, of course, I loved. She asked me to pretend I was a princess and things like that, which I had no problem doing *(laughs)*.

CALLWOOD: Every little girl is a princess.

KAIN: Yes. So after I did this, she said that they would like to take me at the school. I was a little too young, but they recommended a teacher in Mississauga, where we were moving to. I'm ever grateful to Betty Carey because I never would have had a career as a classical dancer if she had not guided us to that school.

CALLWOOD: I once talked to Betty Oliphant about what she looked for. She said that some children will never be dancers, no matter how much they yearn, because they simply don't have the right body build.

KAIN: Did she mean classical dancers?

CALLWOOD: Yes.

KAIN: The physical requirements are very specific for a classical dancer.

CALLWOOD: The foot has to be just so. There's a certain way the leg has to grow and if it doesn't grow that way, it's not likely you're going to have a career as a ballet dancer. So she's looking at anatomy, isn't she?

KAIN: She is. They look at parents, too, to get an idea of how your body is likely to develop. It's very important to have a certain physique for classical ballet. But there are other things that you don't see at first glance, such as drive, determination, and musicality. You can only find out about those sort of things by working with students. I think that's why they now have a year-long program at the ballet school where they look at the students on Saturday mornings. They take lessons and it's a year-long audition, so the teachers get to work with them and see what else they're capable of. Some people have the best bodies, the body everyone would ever want for classical dance, but they don't have the determination. They aren't workers. They don't have what it takes to become classical dancers, even though their bodies are perfect.

CALLWOOD: I gave a talk at the National Ballet School a few weeks ago. All the students sat on the floor in the gymnasium with their backs perfectly straight. All these tiny people sat with perfect poise. But they're boarders and that must be lonely for a small child.

KAIN: That was hard for me. I remember a couple of years of extreme homesickness. I would call home crying and say that I missed everybody. My parents would say, "Come home, forget ballet school." However, as soon as I was faced with that decision, I would always decide I wanted to dance. I think this really became clear when I was about 15 and we were going to Winnipeg for the summer vacation. We often did this because both my parents are from Winnipeg and have relatives there. That year I wanted to do summer school at the National Ballet

School, but my parents said, "No. This summer you're going to just be a regular kid. You're going to come with the family and spend the summer with us. Then you'll see how you really feel about dancing." That did it. After being away from ballet school for two months, I became determined to have a career as a dancer. I really knew that's what I wanted. Having time away is good for us sometimes. The times that I've been injured in my career or off for whatever reason make me hunger to dance again. You come back with sort of renewed determination to do it.

CALLWOOD: You must have been still a little overweight when you joined the National Ballet School because there's a famous story about Betty Oliphant saying to you, you've got two weeks to lose — how many pounds?

KAIN: Ten at least, and I did it.

CALLWOOD: For an audition for Celia Franca, who was a tough auditioner.

KAIN: Yes, and that was to join the National Ballet Company, which was everything I wanted.

CALLWOOD: Were you able to lose that weight without making yourself so weak you couldn't dance?

KAIN: I guess I was so nervous about the audition that the adrenaline just took over. I remember I had eaten only lettuce and tomatoes for two weeks. It was pretty boring but it worked. However, as soon as Betty told me that I'd been accepted, I rushed to the nearest bakery and bought a dozen cookies, which is not very good behaviour. I don't recommend it to anyone.

CALLWOOD: Do you still have to watch your weight? Do you still diet?

KAIN: I still have to watch my weight. I think you really have to be too thin in life to look good on the stage. Also because I am tall, it's very hard for people to lift me, and I don't want to be responsible for them having injured backs.

CALLWOOD: Giving all your partners a hernia would be bad for your reputation.

KAIN: Yes *(laughs)*. So I do watch my weight.

CALLWOOD: Then a magical thing happened, which is so corny nobody would write about it in fiction. You were an understudy and then you had your moment. Many people must know what happened in Arizona, but tell the story anyway.

KAIN: I wasn't really even the understudy. I was in the *corps de ballet* and we were going on a big tour of the States. Veronica [Tennant] had injured her back and the company could not afford a guest artist. They couldn't afford to bring someone in to do the lead in *Swan Lake*, so Celia had to look in the ranks. Now, she could have picked another principal dancer or even a soloist, but she decided to give me the chance. I'd just like to set the record straight, because so many people think that Rudolf Nureyev discovered me. It was actually Celia who gave me my first opportunity and I was already a principal dancer when Rudolf came to the company, although I was a very young principal dancer.

CALLWOOD: How did you know the part?

KAIN: I didn't know the part. I had to learn it in a very short time. I think I had three weeks before we left on the tour, which is a very short time to build the kind of stamina needed for a lead part. However, I did manage to have it by the time the show came around.

CALLWOOD: Oh, it's terribly straining to dance *Swan Lake*, isn't it?

KAIN: It is and especially when you're nervous. It's one thing to get through it in the studio, where you're a little calmer, but when you suddenly have 2,000 people looking at you, you feel exhausted before you even go out, because nerves are very draining. They really make you feel weak. Fortunately, I had a very experienced partner. He is now a character artist in the company. His name is Hazaros Surmeyan, and he had already danced the ballet many times with many people.

CALLWOOD: He must have thought, I have this kid now.

KAIN: He had this kid. He also had had knee surgery not long before that, so he was being careful himself. Before we left on the tour, I had lost a lot of weight through nervousness. So I was quite weak at the time of the performance, and when I got to the fourth act, my legs started to buckle. I was like a colt. I would go to do something and my leg would collapse under me like a noodle. Hazaros would sweep me off my feet and do a lift with me. I'll always remember that.

CALLWOOD: He had to improvise with the choreography.

KAIN: Yes. He had to make a few changes in the last act because my legs were crumbling, which was a scary sensation.

CALLWOOD: *Swan Lake* is a difficult ballet for any dancer. Having to dance the parts of both the Black Swan and the White Swan in the *pas de deux* scene is especially challenging.

KAIN: That's the fun part, though. I enjoy the challenge of playing both roles and making them work so that people have to check their programs to see if it really is the same person. The hard part is the technical challenge of it.

CALLWOOD: Is it the same person? The woman in black comes on so strong she seems a different woman. Then you get this lovely thing in white floating through the room.

KAIN: That's the challenge. It's also a challenge to take an old ballet like that with a really ridiculous story and per-form it in such a way that people can relate the things that happen in it to real and important experiences in their lives, such as betrayal and losing someone you love and having to be strong at the end. *Swan Lake* touches on all those things as does *Giselle*.

CALLWOOD: It's another corny ballet.

KAIN: Yes, it is incredibly corny, but the emotions that are there are so real, such as the strength of love that outlasts death. All of those things are important. That's why we still do them. That's why they still work.

CALLWOOD: You've done many of the classics, the white ballets. Do you do much contemporary dance?

KAIN: I do and I enjoy it. I love the challenges of contemporary, too. There's never any story. The symbolism is very strong, but you're never quite sure if what you see is what the choreographer meant you to see.

CALLWOOD: I don't know what they're doing most of the time. When I see Dancers for Life — you were in the last performance, the benefit for the AIDS Committee of Toronto — I see a little bit of what people are doing right across the country. That's exciting. But their performances make me think how inventive dance has become. I've always loved the classics best.

KAIN: It's fascinating for me to be part of something like that and to get a chance to see such a cross section of people. The atmosphere backstage is really interesting. They watch us putting those funny shoes on our feet, you know and —

CALLWOOD: They're all barefoot.

KAIN: Exactly and we're always arguing about the surface of the stage, because what's slippery for me is sticky for them. That's always a problem, but otherwise it's really fun. It's nice that the whole dance community gets together to do something for people that's very important.

CALLWOOD: Now I have this heartbreaking story to tell you. I had a dance teacher who had me on pointes when I was six.

KAIN: Oh, dear.

CALLWOOD: They used to put lambswool in the toe and my toes would bleed into the lambswool. So every time I see you or anyone on pointes, my heart begins to hurt because I still think that it must be terribly painful to be right on your toe.

KAIN: Well, it is. But we now have several ways of making it considerably less painful. I wish I'd discovered some of them a lot sooner. Thank goodness, we have a foot doctor, a Dr. Walpole. He's been coming to the company since before I joined. He is very good at inventing ways to help us avoid injuries. For instance, I used to get soft corns between my toes because they were always being squeezed. So he brought in these foam things that fit on your toes and keep them apart. Now I no longer have that problem. We also use Second Skin, which you may have heard of because runners and bicyclists use it. They use it on their feet and hands when they get blisters. We tape Second Skin onto our toenails to keep the pressure off them so they don't bruise. Bruising is the worst thing. Blisters are bad, but bruising is even worse because you can't even stand the weight of the sheets on your toes at night. It's too much pressure.

CALLWOOD: Do you still dance if your toenails are bruised?

KAIN: I haven't had much bruising since I discovered this. It takes a little more time to get your feet ready to put them in those shoes. Everyone has different kinds of problems with their feet, but there are a number of different ways of preventing such injuries.

CALLWOOD: Is that why I see dancers sewing the toes of their shoes? What are they doing?

KAIN: That's to make their shoes last longer. Or sometimes if the shoe is a little crooked, they sew to level it out.

CALLWOOD: Do you only wear a pair of shoes once?

KAIN: I usually only wear mine once. In a performance sometimes I'll go through two or three pairs, but I will have broken them in to a certain point beforehand. I wear them for rehearsals to get them to just the right point of softness. If they're too hard, I can't control what I'm doing very well and I'm more likely to slip.

CALLWOOD: Do you knead them to make them softer?

KAIN: I actually dance on them and they take the shape of my foot more. Then they feel more comfortable and I can control the amount of force I need. If they're brand-new, they tend to be very slippery, which can be a little frightening. So we all have our own ways of breaking in our shoes and protecting our feet when we dance on pointes. It's a lot less painful now, but it's still something that takes a lot of getting used to. I think dancers have very high pain thresholds, especially the women, because of this.

CALLWOOD: Well, you're putting all your weight on your big toe.

KAIN: Well, it depends. I mean if you have toes that are more of one length, the weight is distributed more evenly.

CALLWOOD: What are your toes like? Do they go back?

KAIN: No, they're pretty square. I have pretty square feet, which I think is a good thing, but then more toes get bruised.

CALLWOOD: I look at Betty Oliphant, who is now suffering greatly from arthritis, as you know. She says that the arthritis has resulted from dance injuries she had earlier. She thinks she's paying the piper now. You're the president of something called Dancers Transition.

KAIN: The Dancer Transition Centre, yes.

CALLWOOD: Does that help people whose bodies have been worn out too soon by dance?

KAIN: Not necessarily. That's the interesting part of it. A lot of people have to stop dancing much sooner than they expected to for various reasons. Some people get injured very early on in their careers. I've known a lot of people like that. They either have a fall or a part of their physique just doesn't hold up to the kind of stresses that they've been placing it under. It can be an accident; it can be just normal wear and tear, but I've seen a lot of people who have had to stop dancing as early as 21. Other people just discover that they're disillusioned with the lifestyle. It's too hard; they don't make enough money.

CALLWOOD: It's lonely, too, isn't it?

KAIN: It's all of these things. It's been wonderful for me, but it's not for everybody. And these people decide that it's time to change their lives. However, all they've ever done is dance. All they know is dance. All they're trained for is dance.

CALLWOOD: They're like athletes.

KAIN: They go through a hard time letting go of dancing. It's a kind of grieving process. Then they have to get back on their feet, and they usually have no money saved because they never made any to start with. They often can't afford to go back to school, which is what many of them need to do to start a new life. They're not always sure what they'll be good at or what they should do, so we help them. We talk to them. We guide them to the right counsellors. I don't do it personally. I help raise money for the organization. We've helped hundreds and hundreds of dancers across this country, which is just amazing. I'm very proud of it. They go back to school. They become all sorts of things and they're good at it. They're really good at it because they're disciplined, hardworking, courageous people. I'm speaking of people who are all different ages.

CALLWOOD: Don't dancers go through a kind of physical attrition after a long career? Isn't there a creaky old age in store for most of them?

KAIN: I think it depends on how you look after yourself. We know so much more now about how to do this. Dancers have not been well looked after in the past. Look at the way they look after racehorses, and I know they make a lot more money.

CALLWOOD: Do you remember *They Shoot Horses, Don't They?*

KAIN: Well, yeah. That's the sad part of a racehorse's life. One of my sisters used to ride racehorses and train them. She would tell me it's very scientific. This is also the case with athletes, because they can only perform for a very short time and a lot is riding on their careers. Their coaches know so much about how they should take care of themselves. Well, dance training is slowly catching up with athletic training. There's still a lot more to know, but we have already learned a lot. Consequently, we are taking better care of ourselves. We finally have a physiotherapist at the National Ballet. However, we don't have any of the fancy equipment the hockey players have. Their trainers know exactly what's wrong with them. So they can treat them immediately and get them back on the ice as fast as possible.

CALLWOOD: With Novocaine.

KAIN: Well, that's not a great idea. But they really can help them recover faster from their workouts. They can discover injuries early on before they become chronic and they can treat them. They can strengthen the athletes so that they don't have these problems again. With dancers, the situation is only beginning to catch up. We fought very hard to have a physiotherapist and a masseur to help prevent injuries that you get from muscles being overused.

CALLWOOD: It's high time you had access to those kinds of professionals. What about the emotional demands of a dancer's career? You experienced a depression towards the end of the 1970s after you'd been on tours all over the world and had starred with the Bolshoi Ballet and the Paris and New York ballets. You've certainly come to grips with that dip in your mood. You understand it and have pulled yourself out of it.

KAIN: Oh, well, it was a long process. I had to do a lot of work. I think that I had been very one-sided in my life. It was time for me to deal with that and to have a life. You know that expression. We laugh, but I didn't have a life at all.

CALLWOOD: You were a dancer.

KAIN: I was just a dancer. It was a wonderful, wonderful time for me. However, at some point I realized that there was a lot missing in my life. It was my own fault, but I didn't really know how to go about changing it or even really understand what was missing. There were many things that I had never taken the time to even think about.

CALLWOOD: So you took care of yourself for a while.

KAIN: I took care of myself, but unfortunately I had let things slide so far that it was quite apparent that I was a very unhappy person. I guess that's what happens, though. Finally, I was forced to come to terms with my life.

CALLWOOD: But you have such an ability to be a pleasant person, not that it's conjured up out of nothing. You always seem to be totally poised and comfortable, whatever situation you're in. Yet your mum says you used to be incredibly shy and anxious to please in a way that was almost harmful to you.

KAIN: Yes, I was a terribly insecure, shy child. If I saw any strangers approaching the house, I'd run to my bedroom and hide. Once I remember being forced to come down and say hello to people who'd come over to visit. I don't know why, but it was torture for me to come down and say hello.

CALLWOOD: Yes, I know what that feels like.

KAIN: I still think that I am a very shy person. I don't enjoy big parties. I'm happy being home alone.

CALLWOOD: You and your husband are living a very quiet life for people who are celebrities. I don't see you much at openings or anything. But you don't have much time, I suppose.

KAIN: Part of it is that all of that is exhausting and I only have enough energy for what I do. I can't go out and party and see this and that, although I try to see as much as I can. I want to know what's going on in our city.

CALLWOOD: You've done all the big roles haven't you?

KAIN: Well, *The Taming of the Shrew* is coming up in February. I'm very excited about that because this is a role I've always wanted to do.

CALLWOOD: You're going to be Kate.

KAIN: Yes.

CALLWOOD: That role gives women a lot of problems.

KAIN: I know.

CALLWOOD: Do you get to wear a great costume? I love the clothes in ballet.

KAIN: Oh, Susan Benson is doing brand new costumes and sets for *The Taming of the Shrew*, which are going to be spectacular. I've already had a few fittings. I think it's just going to be a really comedic evening, and people are going to have a good time.

CALLWOOD: You've been dancing now with the National Ballet for 20 years. Didn't you have an anniversary that was called Celebrating Kain, which was magical?

KAIN: I've been with the company for 21 years now.

CALLWOOD: You've had a couple of reunions with Frank Augustyn. You danced with him in *Romeo and Juliet*. Was it wonderful to be back together with him?

KAIN: Oh, that was so wonderful. It brought back so many memories.

CALLWOOD: It's still there for both of you?

KAIN: It was in the partnering definitely. Because Frank had flown in only the day before the performance and I was hurting from the season, we didn't really rehearse. I thought, oh dear, this is going to be a disaster. You could just imagine it. But when we got out there and the music started, we just went back in time. It just all came together again. I remember thinking as we were doing it that there was hardly time to think about anything, but it was such a delight to feel his coordination, his work with his hands, and his timing again. It was magic.

CALLWOOD: The audiences have talked about it ever since. Everyone who was there thought it was a really special moment.

KAIN: Oh, it definitely was for me. I think it was so lovely that the company paid Frank a tribute. He deserved it because he gave a lot to the National Ballet of Canada.

CALLWOOD: Well, Dame Margot danced into her 50s, and her performances became richer and more beautiful. So what are the limitations that age imposes? What are the things that remain to be explored? What are the ups and downs of the aging process?

KAIN: I don't know.

CALLWOOD: Are you 40 or 41 now?

KAIN: I'm 40 years old and I feel like the payoff for all those years is just now.

CALLWOOD: It's all come together.

KAIN: Yes. I've never enjoyed dancing so much as I do now. I don't like absolutely every performance, but I finally feel like I have my nerves under control and I know what I'm doing. I can get some pleasure out of what I do rather than just being so tormented about it. But the irony of what we do is that I don't know how long I can continue to do it and enjoy it, because I have lots of aches and pains. I've always had lots of them.

CALLWOOD: Is there more pain now?

KAIN: Yes, it's harder now. It takes longer to warm up, and all of those things. But the payoff is greater. What I've lost a bit of in one area, I've gained in another. I don't know how long I'll be able to continue; I just take it year by year. I certainly hope I'll be able to step down gracefully when it's time.

CALLWOOD: Veronica did it well.

KAIN: She did it very gracefully. I admire her so much for that.

CALLWOOD: But it doesn't have to just stop, does it? Can't you do just a little bit?

KAIN: Oh, maybe. It depends on roles and opportunities. It's very hard to stay in good condition, though, if you're only doing a show here and there. It's very hard to be motivated to work that hard.

CALLWOOD: Do you work every day?

KAIN: Yes. Well, not every day. I take at least one day off a week, sometimes two.

CALLWOOD: Otherwise you're in rehearsal?

KAIN: Yes. I have this list in my mind, though, of all the things I'm going to do when I have time. I'm sure everyone does.

CALLWOOD: What's on your list?

KAIN: Reading. I love to read. I even buy the books I intend to read and pile them up. I am someone who could sit for six hours in a row and not put a book down. I will read all night. I get so involved that I only let myself do it when I can catch up on my sleep and everything. I also would like to learn how to drive.

CALLWOOD: You don't drive a car?

KAIN: No, I don't. It's kind of embarrassing. There are so many things like that that I just never took the time to do because I was so involved in dancing.

CALLWOOD: Do you plan to get fat?

KAIN: I don't think I want to get fat, but I wouldn't mind putting on a few pounds. I would enjoy that. I have a long list.

CALLWOOD: I hope it's quite a while before you get to it, if you don't mind my saying so. But that's just selfish. Thanks, Karen.

KAIN: Thank you.